COLLINS GEM

SCOTS

Text by Carol P. Shaw
Illustrations by Alastair Fyfe

HarperCollins*Publishers*

HarperCollins Publishers
P. O. Box, Glasgow G4 0NB

First published 1995
Reprint 10 9 8 7 6 5 4 3 2 1

The Famous Scots on the cover are (clockwise
from top right-hand corner) Robert Burns,
Sean Connery, Flora Macdonald, John Logie Baird,
and Mary, Queen of Scots.

ISBN 0 00 470809 1

Printed in Italy by Amadeus S.p.A.

Introduction

What is a Scot? The answer would depend on who was being asked the question, but for the purposes of this book it is assumed that a Scot is someone who was born in Scotland. As always, of course, exceptions exist for every rule. There are those who were not Scots-born but without whom no book of Scottish lives would be complete, from Bonnie Prince Charlie – an Italian by birth – to the Irish St Columba, who gave his most productive years to Scotland. And there are others still who, like Alexander Graham Bell, qualify by birth, but achieved most in other lands, most notably North America.

Even within this relatively narrow framework, hundreds of Scots could have been included in the book. The ability of such a small country on the north-western fringes of Europe to produce so many remarkable people is extraordinary. Most, although by no means all, are to Scotland's credit; the occasional one to its shame. And women, whose lives so often pass unnoticed, are conspicuously under-represented.

Those who do appear have been chosen for a wide variety of reasons, but the one thing common to all is that their lives were, or are, interesting. Basing a series of small biographies on entertainment value rather than on worldly achievement has ensured that the book is packed with interesting people and stories from a wide range of personalities, achievements and professions. Medicine and engineering are two areas which are particularly well represented. And at the risk of further reinforcing national stereotypes, it must be emphasised that, at a cover price which breaks down at less than 3p per Scot, this book gives excellent value for money.

Ralph Abercromby
1734–1801
British army general

Early life   Ralph Abercromby was born at Menstrie near Tullibody. Although he studied law at Edinburgh and Leipzig, his preference was for a career in the army, and he purchased a commission in the Third Dragoon Guards in 1756.

Personal bravery   In a military career spanning some 40 years, Abercromby rose to the rank of major-general and distinguished himself in theatres of war as diverse as Flanders, the West Indies and north Africa, where his outstanding personal bravery – often taking place against a background of bumbling incompetence from his superiors – won him instant and enduring fame at home. He was regarded as one of the best generals of his day, but his greatest successes were not won on the battlefield, but in his reforms of the British army itself.

Army reforms   After its defeats in the War of the American Revolution (1775–1783), the British army was ill-disciplined, demoralised and possessed of an officer class in which high rank was often the result of political influence rather than of talent. Abercromby was all too aware of these shortcomings, and in all his commands he sought to improve the lot, and therefore the morale, of the common soldier, as well as the professionalism and dedication of his officers, often against the tradition and accepted practice of the time.

Achievements   By the time of his death from wounds which he received in the battle against the French at Aboukir Bay in 1801, Abercromby was being credited with having regenerated the spirit of discipline and military prowess in the army. In the talented officers he brought on, such as John Moore and Arthur Wellesley, the future Duke of Wellington, he had laid the foundations for future British successes against Napoleon.

Robert Adam
1728–92
Architect

Architecture in the family   Robert Adam was born into a
Kirkcaldy family. His father, William (1689–1748) was a success-
ful architect, and he and his three brothers, John, James and
William, all followed his father into the profession.

Italian influence   Robert was educated at Edinburgh University
where he was one of a glittering group of contemporaries including the philosopher David **Hume** and the economist Adam
Smith. The continued success of the family business, run by the
eldest brother, John, after their father's death meant that Robert
could go to Europe on the Grand Tour to continue his education
– the fashion among sons of the well-to-do. His experience in
Italy, where he spent much time from 1754 to 1758, had a for-
mative influence on his ideas, which subsequently were neoclassi-
cal in style. Diocletian's palace at Spalatro made a particular
impression on him; while classical architecture at home was used
in the design of public buildings, here was an example of its use
in a domestic context.

Chequered business career   The publication of his sketches of the
palace on his return quickly established Adam's name in London,
where he set up practice on his return. He was joined by his brother, James, in 1760. Much of their work initially consisted of interiors and furniture design, which they believed should be of a unified style; for example, one of their classical designs for furniture
was for a sideboard with urn-shaped knife boxes. They are also
said to have been the first to come up with the idea of giving a
unified facade to a group of individual private buildings – as in
Portland Place, whose design is credited mainly to James. They
almost over-reached themselves at the end of the 1760s, however,
when their speculative development of the Adelphi (the Greek

word for 'brothers') area off the Strand grew so much in cost that it came close to ruining them. It was finally disposed of by lottery in 1773, leaving their firm solvent once more.

Achievements and work Adam eventually rose to distinguished heights: in 1762 he became royal architect, a post he resigned six years later when he was elected MP for Kinross. His part-time political work did not get in the way of his designs, however, and he and his brothers are credited with the design of many beautiful buildings throughout the British Isles. Perhaps the best extant grouping of his work can be seen in the New Town in Edinburgh, where he designed the magnificent Charlotte Square, a fitting culmination to the development of the New Town in 1791. Register House and the Old College of Edinburgh University, as well Culzean Castle in Ayrshire, are other famous examples of his work.

Legacy Robert Adam was buried in Westminster Abbey, but his reputation fell away after his death, and only in relatively recent times has his genius once more been recognised. A sense of proportion, unity of style and elegance are the distinguishing features of the Adam brothers' work.

Alexander III
1241–1286
King of Scots

Lineage Alexander III was a direct descendant of the first Scots king, Kenneth MacAlpin, and was the last of the Celtic kings. He succeeded his father, Alexander II, in 1249 and was married at 10 years of age to Margaret, daughter of Henry III of England. The couple had a daughter and two sons.

A Golden Age From the stormy years of the 14th century Alexander's reign was looked back on as a golden age. He was a strong ruler and the kingdom was at peace, the economy was healthy and the country was independent, governed by its own institutions and laws. Alexander was strong enough to fend off English interference and he also ended the Norse threat in Scotland, defeating the Norwegians at the Battle of Largs in 1263. The consequent Treaty of Perth in 1266 secured both the Hebrides and the Isle of Man for Scotland.

Dynastic disasters But Alexander's catalogue of family misfortunes were to drag Scotland into a struggle for its very existence. His wife died in 1275 and his son, David, in 1281. His daughter, Margaret, married Erik II of Norway but died in 1283 giving birth to their daughter, also Margaret. The death in 1284 of his 20-year-old son, Alexander, left him without a male heir, so in 1285 he married again. On a stormy night in 1286 the king was riding from Edinburgh to rejoin his new wife at Kinghorn. He became separated from his guides when his horse missed its footing and threw him to his death over a cliff. The queen gave birth to a stillborn baby seven months later. The little Princess Margaret of Norway was recognised as his successor but the poor child also died on the voyage to her new kingdom in 1290. The dynastic and legal shambles which ensued was resolved only with **Robert I**'s victory in 1314.

Margot Asquith
1864–1945
Society figure and wit

Family Emma Alice Margaret Tennant, known as Margot, was born in Peeblesshire, the eleventh child of the Liberal industrialist Sir Charles Tennant. (He himself was the grandson of the chemist Charles **Tennant** who established the family's fortunes.) She was the most brilliant of an extraordinary family and first came to society's notice during her 'coming out' season of 1881 when, despite her lack of conventional good looks, she was a sensation.

Friends The 'unteachable and splendid' Margot had little formal education. She was a member of a *beau monde* group of intellectuals and aesthetes known as 'The Souls', and numbered among her friends the foremost politicians of the day, including Rosebery, Balfour (who were both rumoured to be involved with her romantically) and Gladstone, as well as figures such as Virginia Woolf.

Marriage to Asquith But in 1894, after pondering his proposal for three years, she married Herbert Asquith, then Liberal Home Secretary and later Prime Minister. Asquith was coolly intellectual and rational while Margot was whole-hearted and instinctive, but despite their temperamental differences and some difficulties, the marriage of these two extremes was a basically happy one. Asquith, by then in his early 40s, had been married before, and Margot took on a ready-made family of five. She had seven children of her own, but tragically only two survived infancy. The pregnancies, all difficult, ruined her health and left her prey to bouts of near-total sleeplessness.

Vivaciousness and wit Margot's life-loving personality shone out like a beacon, making her the leader of society and its most influential figure throughout her life. She was generous, witty, gregarious and a natural show-off. She was also forthright in expressing her opinions, saying, 'When I hear nonsense talked, it makes me

physically ill not to contradict'. When such directness was coupled to wit, however, it could be cruel; when her name was mispronounced by the American actress Jean Harlow, Margot announced before the assembled company, 'The "t" is silent, as in "Harlow".' She knew all the famous people of her day and her magnetic personality and genuine good nature meant she was on good terms with most. One exception was the poisonous Lord Alfred Douglas, former friend of Oscar Wilde, who subjected the Asquiths to an obsessive hate campaign over their friendship with Robert Ross, Wilde's literary executor.

Records of her life Margot published a series of indiscreet and highly entertaining autobiographies and reminiscences in which she recorded apparently verbatim conversations with politicians, society figures and royalty, as well as her opinions of almost all, with the notable exception of Kitchener, whom she hated and distrusted and of whom she said that if he was not a great man, he was, at least, a great poster.

Dugald Baird
1899–1986
Pioneer of maternity and neonatal care

Education and early career Dugald Baird was born in Greenock in 1899. He graduated in medicine from Glasgow University, and it was his experience in the maternity wards and in attendance at births in the wealthy and the poor homes of the city which shaped his thinking and dictated the course of his career.

Improvements in maternity care Baird was appointed to the chair of midwifery at Aberdeen in 1937, and set about further researching his ideas on the causes of maternal and infant mortality. With aid from the Medical Research Council he established a research unit for obstetric medicine, of which he was the first director. Sociologists, statisticians and dieticians were brought into the department to study the reasons for the discrepancy in mortality rates among mothers and babies who came from poor backgrounds, and those who were well-off. His methods and findings have had a huge influence on the conduct of maternity care to the present day.

Advocation of contraception Baird was also a passionate believer in what he called the Fifth Freedom; as well as freedom from evil, war, famine and disease, women should also have freedom from the tyranny of excessive fertility. He advocated access to contraception for all, and was in the forefront of the movement for reform of the abortion law in the 1960s. He retired as professor in 1965, having received a knighthood for his services in 1959.

His legacy Baird was one of several Scots – such as John **Boyd Orr** and Nora **Wattie** – who were dealing with and successfully tackling the same types of poverty-related problems at this time. He was also one of a succession of Scots obstetricians passionately devoted to improving the health and life expectancy of their poorest patients.

John Logie Baird
1888–1946
Pioneer of television and inventor

Sickly childhood The son of a Helensburgh minister, John Logie
Baird was shy and sickly as a child and as a young man. He studied electrical engineering at Glasgow University but ill-health
forced him out of his first job with an electricity company and dis-
qualified him from military service in 1914.

Fantastic inventions Finding it difficult to hold down regular
employment, he became a professional inventor, devising such
wonderful failures as a process to manufacture synthetic dia-
monds. His design for an all-seasons sock did make a profit,
which he used to emigrate in search of a healthier climate, first to
the Caribbean and then to the USA. But one attempt to make
money, by opening a jam factory during his time abroad, was des-
tined to failure when his factory was invaded by ants who carried
away much of the sugar.

Television After returning to Britain, Baird began to develop his
ideas for the transmission of pictures. The idea of separating
images into lines was an established one, and by 1924 Baird was
able to transmit a flickering image over a short distance. He
demonstrated his new invention at a fair in Selfridge's. His real
breakthrough came in 1925, however, when he devised a 30-line
system in which pictures were scanned mechanically by means of
a spinning disc with holes through which light passed. Baird gave
the first real demonstration of television to members of the Royal
Institute at his attic workshop in Soho on 26 January 1926, by
transmitting pictures from one room to another.

He now devoted his energies entirely to the development of his
invention. He raised money for research, built a transmitter and
started his own TV station, the first in the world. His efforts
attracted the attention of the BBC, who in 1929 made the first

television broadcast, provided by Baird's company. He broadcast regularly for the BBC, providing the first sight and sound broadcast and the first outside broadcast, of the 1931 Derby.

Other teleophonic inventions

But Baird was not a businessman, and failed to attract the capital to develop his ideas. He also missed the potential for the development of electronic television provided by the cathoderay tube, and a system using this and developed by Marconi was chosen in preference to Baird's mechanical system by the BBC in 1937. Baird continued his researches until his death, making further refinements to his system, experimenting with colour, large-screen, 3-D and telephone television, and stereophonic sound. His phonovision system, using video signals on a disc to store images, was a forerunner of the compact-disc video.

His personal success

Baird was never a rich man, and stated latterly that he should have sold his invention for others to develop, as **Bell** had done. Yet it was his consuming passion, and was far more important to him than the mere pursuit of wealth: he had been offered over £100,000 for his shares in his television company, but he refused, saying that he would not have been able to sleep at night with such an amount of money. He was a true visionary, whose far-sightedness and drive guided his initially scattergun approach to invention into the development of the most powerful communication tool of the modern era.

J. M. Barrie
1860–1937
Novelist and playwright

James Matthew Barrie was born on 9 May 1860 in Kirriemuir, the ninth child of a weaver. In his lifetime Barrie was a literary giant whose reputation was almost on a par with that of Dickens, although it faded astonishingly quickly after his death.

Early life As a child he wrote for his school's magazine and drama group, in which he also acted. Although he went on to gain a degree at Edinburgh, he had already decided on writing as a career. In 1885, after a short stay in Nottingham where he worked as a journalist, he moved to London and quickly established his reputation, churning out articles and later novels, many portraying a sentimentalised view of Scottish life.

Psychological problems Barrie's psyche seems greatly to have been affected by his stature: he never grew beyond 5 feet 1 inch in height. It was always a source of immense sorrow to him, and he stated that, had he grown to full height, he would not have bothered to write, but would instead have become a ladies' man. Whatever the truth of this statement, it is revealing that Barrie, whose *raison d'etre* was writing, would under any circumstances have considered it unnecessary. It may also help in explaining the affinity which he felt with children: while, on the one hand, he hated to be mistaken for a child when he was a young man, he not only exhibited childish qualities throughout his life, but he felt more at home in the company of children.

Peter Pan Almost all of Barrie's novels and plays were great successes in their time, but it is for *Peter Pan* that he is remembered today. The play about the boy who never grew up has elements which may be difficult for modern children to accept, but the engaging nature of the story has ensured its survival. The character was, according to Barrie, a composite based on five brothers, the Davieses, who were his neighbours in Kensington and whose parents Barrie befriended. The boys' mother and father both died young, and Barrie adopted the children in 1910. His own childless marriage had ended the previous year when his wife, an actress, ran off with a younger man; her affair had been shockingly revealed to the stunned Barrie by his gardener.

Personal tragedies Barrie's life was blighted by the deaths of those close to him: his brother, his mother's favourite child, died when he was 13, and the young James attempted to console his grieving mother by trying to become like his brother in dress and mannerisms. His mother and sister later died, while the fiancé of another sister was killed in a fall from a horse which Barrie had bought as a present for him. The eldest of the Davies boys, George, was killed in the fighting in France in 1915, and the second-youngest, Michael, drowned in 1921, a devastating blow from which the ageing Barrie never fully recovered.

His legacy Barrie's literary contribution was recognised in 1913, when he became a baronet, with the award of the Order of Merit in 1922. His health failed in 1936, and he died the following year, with his writing still enjoying great popularity. Unlike other literary greats he was not buried at Westminster Abbey; instead, at his own request, his last resting place was his native Kirriemuir. Fittingly, royalties from his most famous work, *Peter Pan*, have been awarded in perpetuity to the Great Ormond Street Hospital for Sick Children in London, a gesture of which the ever-generous author would have approved.

15

James Barry

1795–1865

First woman doctor, and male impersonator

James Barry was a woman who appears to have passed in public as a man throughout her entire adult life.

Medical education She was an exceptionally bright child, and it is thought she was sent to Edinburgh University by her male guardian who wished to secure a proper education for her. In 1812, when medicine was still closed to women, she became the first to graduate in medicine (albeit dressed as a man). She joined the army as a hospital assistant in 1813.

Army career Barry served in Malta and the Cape where she worked in the leper colonies and tried to improve conditions for the slaves. She was the first recorded physician to perform a caesarean which saved the life of both mother and baby. By the time she retired in 1859 she was a highly skilled and respected army surgeon and had attained the rank of inspector general .

Personality and relationships It is believed that during her career she had an affair with the governor of the Cape colony, Sir Charles Somerset. In 1819 she met Lord Albermarle who described an 'effeminacy in [Barry's] manner which he was always striving to overcome. His style of conversation was greatly superior to that one usually heard at a mess table in those days.' She was belligerent by nature, and fought a duel in Cape Town in 1819. During her career she also met Florence Nightingale; the two seem to have been mutually antipathetic.

Discovery of her secret On her death her secret, never suspected by either her landlady or her servant, was discovered. Her body bore the marks of childbirth. It is interesting to speculate on Barry's motives, but it may simply be that she felt she could do most good in the profession in which she was qualified and that required continuing the charade her guardian initiated.

Sawney Bean

Lived in the late 13th and early 14th century
Cannibal

Background and family Although not a great deal is known for certain of his early life, Sawney Bean is believed to have been born in East Lothian in the late 13th century, and was a tanner by trade. He became the notorious leader of a savage family over 45 members strong who settled in a cave at Bennane Head three miles north of Ballantrae in Ayrshire. The Bean family lived by robbing and murdering passing travellers, and then eating their remains.

Horrors of his cave Over a period of six years there had been reports of travellers in the Ballantrae area going missing and never being seen again. But the Beans' crimes were only brought to light when one of their intended victims managed to escape and reported to the authorities the terrors he had experienced and the extent of the horrors he had seen in the cave at Bennane Head. The information was brought to the attention of **James I**, who rode out personally to supervise the capture of Sawney Bean and his family, and their subsequent transportation to Edinburgh. When the Beans' seaside cave was finally investigated, the gruesome finds inside included the pickled limbs of the family's victims – provision for future meals – as well as their clothes, money and weapons. It is believed that 37 people had died at their hands. The family were also discovered to be living in incest, with their children the issue of in-breeding.

The family's executions The Beans were not tried in the capital for their crimes, but were instead summarily sentenced to death. The men of the family were executed by mutilation at Leith, while the women were burned.

Alexander Graham Bell
1847–1922
Inventor of the telephone

Family work in elocution Alexander Bell was born on 3 March 1847. Although his most famous invention was the telephone, his life's work was dedicated to improving systems of communication for the deaf and for deaf mutes. In this he followed in the family tradition, as his father and grandfather were both elocution teachers. Bell was educated at Edinburgh University and at University College, London, and subsequently worked with his father as an assistant. The family would appear to have had a pulmonary weakness, however, and in an attempt to escape the dampness of the British climate, Bell emigrated to Canada in 1870, moving on to the USA the following year.

American career Bell spent a short period as Professor of Vocal Physiology and Elocution in Boston in the early 1870s. During this time he was working on his father's system of 'visible speech', a method of lip-reading for the deaf. He was also engaged in attempts to devise a machine with a receiver and a transmitter which would send sounds telegraphically, and allow deaf people to hear them.

Invention of the telephone This line of research led him into the development of a proto-telephone. Bell was confident enough of the success of his idea to file a patent in February 1876, only days ahead of several of his rivals – a margin so close that he subsequently had to defend his invention in several successful court cases. Finally, on 10 March 1876, the famous first teleophonic transmission: 'Mr Watson, come here; I want you,' was sent by Bell to his assistant.

Its instant success Bell showed his invention at a fair in Philadelphia that year, when he sensationally recited Hamlet's 'To be or not to be' soliloquy over the telephone to the Emperor of

Brazil. He formed the Bell Telephone Company in the following year and became a rich man on the proceeds of its work. Bell was a visionary who realised the potential of his invention, foreseeing a time when people in different parts of the country would be able to speak to one another.

Personal life Bell had continued his teaching of deaf students while he was inventing. One of his most famous students was Helen Keller, the blind and deaf woman who became renowned for her work with the handicapped; she dedicated her autobiography to him. In 1877 he married Mabel Hubbard, another of his students. She remained deaf to the end of her days, but the two enjoyed a close and happy marriage. They had two daughters, although sadly their two sons died in infancy.

Other inventions The family moved to the Canadian Maritimes in 1886, where Bell continued to invent, devising, among other things, flying machines, a universal language, a phonograph, hydrofoils, an iron lung, and a new method of sheep breeding. However, he never had much affection for his most famous invention: 'I never use the beast,' he said of his own telephone, whose bell he stuffed with paper.

Joseph Black
1728–1799
Chemist

Family background and education Born in Bordeaux into a vintner's family, Joseph Black was one of 13 children. He went to Glasgow University to study medicine in 1746, although his interest was already captured by the young science of chemistry. He moved to Edinburgh four years later to complete his studies. Black's MD thesis, presented in 1754, was considered remarkable both for its philosophical style and, more particularly, for its identification for the first time of carbon dioxide.

Glasgow career In 1756 Black was appointed to the chair of anatomy and chemistry at Glasgow, but he felt more confident of his ability to teach medicine, so he and the professor of medicine swopped jobs for the next 10 years. During his time at Glasgow he met and encouraged James **Watt**, passing on to him his most famous advance, the theory of latent heat. Watt used it to good effect in his own work.

Edinburgh life and friendships In 1766 Black was appointed professor of medicine and chemistry at Edinburgh, a position he held until just before his death. Quiet, precise and affable, Black was one of a circle of friends who included Adam **Smith**, David **Hume** and James **Hutton**. He was a fine teacher and attendance at his lectures became a fashionable pastime, helping to popularise the new science of chemistry. But Black declined to pursue his own discoveries, usually delivering his ideas at lectures and rarely publishing his conclusions. This was partly because of his personality and also because of his health, which was poor. He weakened in later years and finally died at table during a meal of bread, prunes and milk-and-water. He divided his estate into 10,000 portions and allocated parts and fractions of parts to relatives according to his perception of their need.

William Blackwood
1776–1834
Publisher

Early successes William Blackwood was born in Edinburgh in November 1776. At 14 years of age he was apprenticed to learn the bookselling trade, and his talents were such that by the time he was 20 he had been employed by an Edinburgh firm to manage the new Glasgow branch of their bookshop. He worked with them for a year before moving on to London to learn the antiquarian trade. By 1804 he had saved enough money to open his own shop back in his native city, selling mainly antiquarian titles, and in a few years he established himself as Scotland's foremost authority in the field.

Blackwood's Edinburgh Magazine Blackwood made a bold move in 1816, when he relocated his premises from Edinburgh's Old Town to Princes Street, then one of the showpiece thoroughfares of the fashionable New Town. On April 1 of the following year he gambled even more, with the publication of his own monthly periodical. Blackwood had long wished to counter the political and literary influence of the Whig *Edinburgh Review*, and, under his editorship, his magazine succeeded in doing that. *Blackwood's Edinburgh Magazine* became one of the foremost periodicals of its day, with its contributors including John Galt, J. G. Lockhart, John Wilson and James **Hogg**. Even more illustrious contributors were later attracted, including the novelists George Eliot and Joseph Conrad. Blackwood was among the first to light upon the idea of publishing stories in serial form, and confined his book-publishing activities mainly to reprinting stories which had first appeared as serials in the magazine. He made contemporary writing available at fairly low cost, while providing a platform for much of the Scottish writing talent of his day.

James Boswell
1740–1795
Writer, and biographer of Dr Johnson

Relationship with his father Born on 29 October 1740, James Boswell was the son of Alexander Boswell of Auchinleck, an advocate. James' parents ensured that their son received a thorough Calvinist upbringing, and the child's exposure to the terrors of hellfire and damnation may in some way account for the personality problems which he displayed as an adult. His relations with his father were strained, and remained so throughout the elder man's life.

Education and escape in Europe At Alexander's insistence James studied law, although intermittently and always reluctantly. After a stay in London in 1763 he was sent to continue his legal studies at Utrecht, and took the opportunity afforded by his distance from Edinburgh to turn the trip into a Grand Tour. Boswell was a social climber with a fancy for the society of the famous whom he would shamelessly toady, usually after thrusting himself into their company. During his European jaunt he made the acquaintance of Voltaire, Rousseau and the Corsican leader, Paoli. Dragged back to Edinburgh at his father's insistence, he finally qualified in 1766, going on to become an indifferent advocate.

Biographer of Johnson During his brief stay in London in 1763 Boswell had met Dr Samuel Johnson. Johnson overcame his renowned hatred of the Scots where Boswell was concerned, and the two became friends in spite of a 31-year age gap. In 1773 Boswell was elected to Johnson's famous Literary Club, and in the same year the pair undertook their famous journey to the Hebrides, an account of which Boswell published in 1785, the year after Johnson's death. In 1791 he published his *Life of Johnson*, in which he proved himself, in Macaulay's words, 'the Shakespeare of biographers'. In fact, Johnson's fame today rests as much on Boswell's biography of him as on his own work.

Sexual promiscuity and marriage

Boswell also wrote his own biography in the form of detailed journals which he kept from the age of 18, and from these his life has gained notoriety. He was sexually promiscuous from his late teens, with innumerable partners including relatives, prostitutes, mistresses, servants and noblewomen. As a consequence, despite his use of sheep's-gut prophylactics, he suffered repeated infection of sexually transmitted diseases, complications from which eventually killed him. He was prone to indulge in excesses of drink and sex for days on end, always followed by remorse. As with the other great diarist, Samuel Pepys, Boswell's confessional and superficially self-analytical mode makes for fascinating reading and is appealing in the way that such personalities invariably are. However, unlike Pepys, Boswell's unfortunate wife, Margaret, was able to read the code in which he recorded his dalliances, and was also forced to endure recitations of them from him. Yet despite his appalling behaviour to her, he was fond of his patient wife, who seems to have represented for him the uncritical parent he never had.

Death
Boswell's personality was always fragile, with behaviour bordering on the manic-depressive, and after his wife's death from TB in 1789, leaving him with five children to care for, he sank into alcoholism and became a pathetic figure in his final years.

Earl of Bothwell
c. 1535–1578
Third husband of Mary, Queen of Scots

Not much is known of the early life of James Hepburn, the fourth Earl of Bothwell. After the death of his father in 1556 he inherited his titles, estates and hereditary offices, including the Lord High Admiralship. He was a vigorous, ambitious man given to reckless behaviour. His relations with Queen **Mary** have been much debated, but without doubt he was her second bad choice in Scottish husbands.

Political manoeuvring Although a Protestant he supported the French regent, Mary of Guise, against other Protestant nobles. This earned him favour with Queen Mary on her return to Scotland in 1561 after her French husband's death. However, his subsequent riotous behaviour saw him exiled from court for four years. He was recalled after Mary's marriage to **Darnley** but did not fully regain her favour until after the murder of her secretary, David Rizzio, in 1566, when he seemed one of the few sympathetic to her cause.

Downfall and horrible death Bothwell came to the fore in 1567: he was involved in Darnley's murder, and in April he abducted the queen. His marriage to Mary caused open revolt, but after her surrender to rebel forces at Carberry Hill on 15 June, Bothwell fled to Orkney and thence to Norway, where he was taken into custody by the country's Danish rulers. His marriage to the queen was annulled in 1570 on the grounds that he had raped her beforehand. From 1573, after the final defeat of Mary's party and through the influence of the Regent Moray, Bothwell was imprisoned in Denmark. He was kept in chains in a dungeon, denied contact with anyone and knew that he would never be released. Under such circumstances it is not surprising that he died insane five years later.

John Boyd Orr
1880–1971
Nutritionist

For a man who did so much to lessen the scale of human suffering, John Boyd Orr's life goes strangely unrecorded in many history books. Born in Kilmaurs, he attended Glasgow University and served with merit in the First World War, winning the MC and the DSO.

Early work in nutrition Boyd Orr was a visionary with, happily and exceptionally, a practical side: he was among the first to recognise the importance of nutrition to health, and he tried to ensure ordinary people received the benefits of his findings. He devised ways of increasing food production, and his work at the Rowett Research Institute in Aberdeen in the early 1940s resulted in the first applications of modern scientific methods to farming.

Findings on diet and health He was a prime mover in an experiment in 1927 to supply free milk to schoolchildren; the result was that differences in stature of poor and better-off children were eradicated, and poorer children's general health improved. The experiment was so successful that it was later adopted on a national scale by the Government. This approach was taken further in the 1930s when he investigated the link between income and food consumption, and concluded that 'a diet completely adequate for health … is reached at an income level above that of 50% of the population' – a finding initially received with hostility and flat disbelief in establishment circles. But it was as a result of Boyd Orr's work that the nation's diet and health improved during the food rationing of the Second World War.

UN career Boyd Orr became first director of the UN Food and Agriculture Organisation and worked successfully to improve food production in the Third World. He was made a peer, and his work won him the Nobel Peace Prize in 1949.

Lord Braxfield
1722–1799
'Hanging' judge

Early legal career Robert MacQueen, later Lord Braxfield, was born in Lanarkshire in 1722. He studied law at Edinburgh and became an advocate in 1744. His speciality was the dry subject of feudal land law, and because of this he was employed by the Crown to help in the forfeiture of Jacobite land after the rising of 1745. He became a Lord of Session in 1776.

His extraordinary behaviour However, it was not his legal achievements but his personality which brought him fame. Braxfield was an intelligent, domineering and brutish bully who was much given to hurling insults and cruel jokes around his courtroom, greatly enjoying any shocked reaction he was able to elicit. He customarily displayed a callous wit when sentencing prisoners to transportation or death. His greatest notoriety was achieved in 1793 at the trials of the Friends of the People, a radical group who brought the ideas of the French Revolution to Scotland. During the trials, one reformer pointed out that Christ himself had been a reformer. 'Muckle he made o' that, he was hangit,' was the judge's reply. Braxfield's lack of even a pretence of impartiality coupled with the viciousness of his sentencing made the Crown disinclined to use him subsequently.

Notoriety Braxfield was immortalised in *Memorials of His Time* by **Cockburn**, who called him 'the Jeffreys of Scotland', a reference to the brutal 17th-century hanging judge. He considered Braxfield's conduct a disgrace, but said it came from 'a cherished coarseness', and not from cruelty, for which he thought him too strong and jovial. **Stevenson**, too, was fascinated by him; while in Samoa he sent home for a copy of Cockburn's book, and used Braxfield as his model for the deliciously appaling Lord Hermiston in his unfinished masterpiece, *Weir of Hermiston*.

Deacon Brodie
1741–1788
Thief

William Brodie led an archetypal double life; by day he was a respected Edinburgh artisan and public figure, and by night a gambler, dissolute liver and burglar.

Public and private lives   Brodie followed his father into the trade of cabinet-making, and became deacon, or head of the Guild of Wrights, entitling him to a seat on Edinburgh's town council. He became a freeman of the city and, to all accounts, was a respectable citizen. But he had acquired a taste for gambling early in life, and spent most evenings in a seedy gaming house in Fleshmarket Close. His losses at the tables, coupled with the need to maintain his two mistresses and five children, left him in difficult financial circumstances. In 1787 he fell in with three villainous characters, with whom he formed a gang. Brodie took advantage of the access to premises he had in his daytime work to make copies of their keys, which his gang then used to effect in a series of baffling robberies in which no clues were ever found.

Caught   Their luck ran out when they were disturbed during a burglary at the Excise office at Chessel's Court in the Canongate. Brodie escaped, but one of his cohorts was to turn king's evidence. Through an unwisely written letter Brodie was traced and arrested in Amsterdam on the point of leaving for America. He was brought back to Edinburgh and tried in the same court where he himself had sat as a jury member only months before. He and an associate were hanged on 1 October 1788.

Jekyll and Hyde   Brodie was another character who caught the imagination of **Stevenson**; he was reputed to have made a bookcase and chest of drawers which stood in the young Lewis' nursery, and *Dr Jekyll and Mr Hyde* is said to have been inspired by Brodie's life.

John Brown
1826–1883
Royal retainer

Career as a gillie John Brown was a crofter's child, born on the Balmoral estate. He began his royal career as a gillie in 1849 during a visit of Queen Victoria and Prince Albert to the estate, when he looked after the queen on an outing. By 1858 he was her personal servant, and in 1864, three years after Albert's death, she took him to England as her groom.

Friendship with the queen Victoria's affection for Brown was obvious; she publicly called him her 'friend and most confidential attendant' and showered him with favour and advancement. For Brown's part, he fitted perfectly the stereotype of the pawky, irreverent, devoted Scottish servant. He saved the queen from personal attack, and rescued her from two carriage accidents. His devotion was coupled with a brusque familiarity; he was heard by a visitor to shout, 'Wumman, can ye no' hold yer head up?' as he helped the queen on with her cloak.

Speculation and gossip Brown's advancement caused jealousy in the royal household and bafflement and disgust among her children, who thought him brutish. Prince Edward ordered the destruction of a small pavilion where his mother and Brown would stop during their walks; Victoria instantly ordered it to be rebuilt, and did not speak to her son for weeks. It is probable that the two stopped there for a session of whisky-drinking, of which they were both fond. However, public speculation about their relationship was outrageous; one rumour reported that the queen had had Brown's son.

Victoria's loyalty Victoria resisted all pressure to distance herself from Brown and was heartbroken when he died. On her own death, a photo of him was among the personal treasures which were placed in her coffin.

James Bruce
1730–1794
Explorer

Early life James Bruce was born into a landed family at Kinnaird in Stirlingshire in 1730. He grew into a tall, vigorous young man with an adventurous spirit. He began the study of law to please his father, but soon abandoned the idea.

Search for adventure Business interests in Spain led to Bruce's learning Arabic and Abyssinian. He came to the notice of the Government and was offered the consulship at Algiers, which he held from 1763 to 1765. It was a dangerous job which he performed well, but he craved a life of travel and discovery.

Explorations in Africa In 1768, having survived a shipwreck, Bruce set off up the Nile to Assouan, sailing through the Red Sea to reach Abyssinia at the start of 1770. He experienced a stroke of luck when he arrived in Gondar, the capital: a smallpox epidemic in the royal palace cleared up, and he was given the credit. He set out with royal blessing to achieve what had become an obsessive goal – the discovery of the source of the Nile. He though he had succeeded, but the river he traced was actually the Blue Nile, the Nile's largest tributary.

Fall from public grace Initially hailed as a hero on his return to Britain in 1774, Bruce soon found the public mood turn against him as he related gory and outlandish tales of the Abyssinians' habits; a particular story of natives cutting flesh to eat from a living animal, was greeted with horror and outrage. Bruce received no honour in recognition of his work and took off in pique to his estates. His epic account of his adventures, *Travels to Discover the Sources of the Nile*, was published in 1790, and despite its readability and popular success it did nothing to revive his reputation. Despite the dangerous life he had led, Bruce died in a fall at home, hurrying downstairs to help a lady into her carriage.

William Bruce
1630–1710
Architect

Architectural legacy William Bruce is generally seen as the founding figure of British Palladianism, a movement derived from the ideas of the 16th-century Italian architect, Andrea Palladio. Palladianism revived the design principles of classical architecture, especially of the Romans, which emphasised harmonious proportions and symmetrical designs, and dovetailed it to the demands of 17th-century life.

Advancement under the Stuarts Born at Blairhall in Fife, William is believed to have been self-educated, and in his youth travelled through England, Holland and France. On his return to Scotland he played an active part in the events leading to the Restoration of the monarchy in 1660, acting as a go-between for Charles II and the Commonwealth leader, General Monck. He was rewarded with a royal appointment in the same year, and in 1668 was created a baronet. The grace and skills evident in his designs led to his appointment as King's Surveyor and Master of Works in 1671, and he was given the important task of restoring Holyrood Palace in Edinburgh, a job which lasted to the end of his tenure in 1678. Throughout 1685 and 1686 Bruce worked to build a mansion on lands he had bought at Kinross, intending it to be a residence for the Duke of York (the future James VII) in case he should be excluded from the throne for his Catholicism. Bruce's very public Jacobite sympathies were to lead to his fall from royal favour after James' deposition in 1689.

His work still extant Several Scottish noble houses still stand as evidence of his talents, including Hopetoun House, which was ultimately completed by William Adam.

Alexander Buchan
1829–1907
Meteorologist

Involvement in meteorology The youngest child of a weaver, Alexander Buchan was born at Kinnesswood in Fife. He became a teacher after graduating from Edinburgh University in 1848, but had to retire from the profession in 1860 because of throat problems. He was appointed secretary to the recently founded Scottish Meteorological Society, beginning work which was to be a consuming interest in his life. The society had been founded by Dr James Stark, a statistician, and its work concentrated on the gathering and interpreting of statistical data drawn from a network of stations across Scotland. Buchan was an enthusiastic convert to the study of meteorology, and became the society's most important figure.

Discoveries Drawn from his observation of the statistics, he put forward the theory which became known as the Buchan Spells – that the British climate undergoes a series of cold and warm periods which fall approximately between certain dates each year. He published his findings in a series of books and papers, the first of which, *The Handy Book of Meteorology*, published in 1867, became a basic text throughout the world. His work over the next 30 years made valuable contributions to every aspect of climatology and meteorology. He also completed studies on the effects of the weather on mortality and the incidence of disease.

Later career Between 1878 and 1906 he was librarian and curator of the museum of the Royal Society of Edinburgh, an appointment which brought him into contact with the foremost Scots scientists of his day. Buchan was always adamant that meteorology should be recognised as the youngest of the sciences.

John Buchan
1875–1940
Writer and statesman

Despite the high political status John Buchan attained, it is for his writing – which he never chose as a career – rather than for his politics that he is remembered today. He was born in Perth, the son of a minister in the Free Church of Scotland.

Political advancement   After studying at Glasgow and Oxford Universities, he was called to the bar in 1901. In the same year he took a government post in South Africa as Britain struggled with its role in the country in the aftermath of the bitter Boer War (1899–1902). Buchan performed his job well, and it proved a stepping stone to political advancement for him. A series of appointments came on his return, including war correspondent for *The Times* during the First World War, and MP. Finally, in 1935, the Prime Minister, Ramsay **Macdonald**, suggested Buchan for the post of Governor General of Canada. His title of Baron Tweedsmuir and his appointment followed the next year. Buchan proved to be a conscientious governor general, travelling widely and familiarising himself with Canada's cultures: he was even made an honorary Indian chief.

Writing career   In tandem with his professional work, Buchan had been writing continually. His first novel, *Prester John*, was published in 1910. Although his interests included poetry and biography – one subject was **Montrose** – his most enduring success came as a writer of adventure stories, or 'yarns', as he termed them. His most famous creation, Richard Hannay, first appeared in *The Thirty-Nine Steps* in 1915, dreamed up while Buchan lay in bed recovering from illness. His novels remain readable and enjoyable today, even though his characters and plots are often too far-fetched for modern tastes.

George Buchanan
1506–1582
Scholar

Success as a scholar George Buchanan was born into a family impoverished by his father's death. At 14 he was sent to Paris by his uncle to study Latin. A subsequent 17-year academic career at Paris and St Andrews was interrupted only by lack of resources, and he became a brilliant scholar of true European standing. This was recognised in 1537 in a royal appointment as tutor to Lord James Stewart (later Earl of Moray), bastard son of **James V**. Buchanan also tutored the king's daughter, Queen Mary, and her son, **James VI**. His talents and his religious conviction were also recognised in 1567 when he became moderator of the new General Assembly, the governing body of the Church of Scotland.

Relationships with Mary and James Despite Buchanan's Protestantism he enjoyed a warm personal relationship with the Catholic Mary, and read Latin to her in the evenings. Yet he turned against her completely when she married the Earl of **Bothwell** after the murder of her husband, **Darnley**. He assisted Moray in having her deposed, and wrote a scurrilous pamphlet against her, based on what he must have known were lies. He never forgave Mary, and when appointed tutor to her four-year-old son he deliberately tried to poison the child's mind against his mother. Although an effective tutor of the young king, he taught by fear: it was later reported of someone reminiscent of Buchanan that James 'ever trembled at his approach'.

Personal failures Many of the deeds done in the name of religion in the 16th and 17th centuries seem extreme today, but even allowing for the reformers' total conviction and utter belief in the righteousness of their cause, Buchanan still comes across as a hard and bitter man, lacking in compassion, and one who did not utilise his obvious talents to their fullest.

Burke & Hare
Burke 1792–1829; Hare 1790–c. 1860
Murderers

Their backgrounds Burke and Hare were not Scottish, but they came spectacularly and gruesomely to public notice in Edinburgh. William Burke was born in County Cork and moved to Scotland around 1818, finding work as a navigator on the Union Canal. In 1827 he moved into a lodging house in Tanner's Close which was kept by William Hare and his wife. Hare had also spent time working on the Union Canal and, like Burke, he was an Irishman, from Londonderry.

Murderous careers Shortly after Burke's arrival, an elderly male resident in the house died; rather than bury him, the two men decided to take advantage of Edinburgh's lucrative resurrection trade, in which newly buried corpses were exhumed and sold to medical schools. They took the body to the prominent anatomist, Dr Robert **Knox**, who paid them £7 10s for it. Such large and easy earnings were too tempting; at Hare's suggestion, the two embarked on an 11-month trail of murder, luring people into the lodging house, getting them drunk and suffocating them. The cadavers were then sold to Knox.

Discovery and downfall But neighbours grew suspicious and reported the pair to the police. A raid on Knox's house revealed in the cellar the body of Burke and Hare's sixteenth victim. But clues were difficult to find as the bodies had no marks on them, and Hare, the more villainous of the two, was persuaded to turn king's evidence against his partner. Burke was tried on Christmas Eve 1828 and hanged in Edinburgh on 28 January 1829 before a crowd of 20,000 who yelled, 'Burke him!' His body later ended up on a dissecting table in a medical school. Hare left for England and is thought to have died destitute in London over 30 years later. Dr Knox was never proved to have known of the murders.

Robert Burns
1759–1796
Poet

Early influences Born in Alloway on 25 January 1759, Robert Burns was the oldest of seven children of a farming family. In his early life and education he gained a familiarity with and a love of folk tales and popular songs. He read poetry and was particularly influenced by the Scots poems of the Edinburgh poet Robert Fergusson. (Burns later paid for a headstone for Fergusson's grave.)

First book and success The years of the mid 1780s were to change Burns' life. In 1784 his father died, and he inherited the farm. But by 1786 he was in financial difficulties: he had made two women pregnant, the farm was not successful, and he was considering taking up a post in Jamaica to make a new start in life. His miserable situation may have been a spur to his writing – some of his most famous work, such as *Holy Willie's Prayer* and *The Cotter's Saturday Night*, was produced around this time. To raise money he published then in Kilmarnock as *Poems, Chiefly in the Scottish Dialect*. The book was a financial and critical success and Burns was persuaded to go to Edinburgh where he became the toast of genteel society as the 'ploughman poet'. His plans for Jamaica were abandoned, and Burns undertook tours around the country during the next two years.

Later work In 1789 he gave up farming, for which he had no talent, moving to Dumfries to become an exciseman. He carried out his duties diligently and conscientiously saw to the education of his children. During these years as well as writing his own poems he worked, unpaid, on two collections of songs: his own, set to traditional tunes, and his reworkings of old ones. The material, among the best he ever produced – was so good as to ensure the survival of many traditional Scots folk songs, and he further enriched the collections with his own compositions, too.

Heavy drinking and physical decline But Burns' health, not good to begin with, was broken by his heavy drinking, and in 1796, after one particularly vigorous bout in the local tavern, he fell asleep outdoors and then contracted rheumatic fever. It was made worse by the prescribed cure – bathing in the chilly waters of the Solway Firth – and Burns died

shortly afterwards, at 37 years of age still a young man.

Sexual potency In keeping with his image as an ardent lover and spectacular progenitor, the last of Burns' children was actually born during his funeral service. This was his seventh living child, although several more had died in infancy. Even though sexual mores in 18th-century rural Scotland were very relaxed, Burns' sexual and procreational achievements seem remarkable. As in all aspects of his life, his feelings were expressed directly in his writings, and his songs and poems of love, such as *Ae Fond Kiss* and *A Red, Red Rose*, are among the most beautiful of their kind in any language. His eldest child, the first of three illegitimate daughters all called Elizabeth, was greeted with the poem *Welcome to a Bastart Wean*. He was a large-hearted figure who with his tolerant and very forgiving wife, Jean Armour (whom he married in 1788) accepted and took responsibility for all his children, legitimate and illegitimate alike.

Political philosophies Despite his romantic and patriotic sympathy for Jacobitism, Burns was a republican who supported the French Revolution of 1789. His radical politics manifested themselves in a championing of the rights of the poor. He was also a Freemason for 15 years, and actively supported the movement which, at that time, espoused humanist and rationalist ideals. His political ideas received their finest expression in the moving *Is There for Honest Poverty* (*A Man's a Man for A' That*). His hatred of religious hypocrisy, too, coming from one who must have experienced it in full measure, was fierce.

Coupling of life and art Burns' poetry and songs are accessible to everyone and are instant in their appeal to the emotions, for he himself was a man of impulsive and generous feeling. He wrote love poems and songs, nature poems, and social, satirical and political works, mainly in Scots dialects, but also in English. His poetry was an extension and integral part of his life, reflecting its every incident and aspect. An incident on 27 February 1792 well illustrated this. Burns was ordered to keep watch on a smuggler's boat in the Solway Firth while his superiors went to Dumfries to fetch reinforcements. During his wait, he sat and composed *The Deil's awa' wi' th' Exciseman*. The boat and its cargo of guns were seized – the poet actually leading the soldiers in their assault on the ship – and sold. Burns himself bought the guns for £3, and promptly sent them to the French legislative body. (Incidentally, this and other too-vocal professions of support for the revolutionaries brought him close to dismissal.)

Undiminished popularity Burns' appeal is enduring and extends internationally and into foreign language editions, and his birthday is celebrated each year by enthusiasts of his life and works.

William Burrell
1861–1958
Shipping magnate and art collector

Early interest in collecting Born in Glasgow, William Burrell was
the third son of a shipowner. The Burrell family firm came to
prominence in 1877 when one of its ships salvaged Cleopatra's
Needle which had been lost in the Bay of Biscay en route to
London. Even as a teenager William dabbled in the art world,
already using his pocket money to buy paintings, much to the
annoyance of his father who felt he should be buying typically
boyish things like cricket bats.

Professional career William had joined his father's business at the
age of 15. As well as successfully running the family firm with his
brother, he collected art throughout his working life. He retired in
1917 after he had made his fortune, intent now on devoting his
time to amassing his collection.

His collection Relying on a trusted network of contacts and spe-
cialist dealers, Burrell travelled throughout Europe in pursuit of
objects, spending £20,000 a year on average between 1911 and
1957 – although some years the figure rose to as much as
£80,000. In 1944 Sir William and Lady Burrell gifted the collection and provision for a gallery to Glasgow, one of the greatest
endowments ever made to a British city. The collection includes
tapestries, stained glass, paintings, ceramics, furniture, silverware,
metalwork, armour and a variety of *objets d'art* – over 8,500
objects in all from Europe and the Near and Far East, represent-
ing virtually every period of artistic endeavour. The Burrell
Collection was finally opened in 1983 in a magnificent new pur-
pose-built gallery and has been one of the top Scottish tourist
attractions ever since. Burrell was knighted for his services to art
in 1927. He died in Hutton Castle near Berwick-on-Tweed, his
home and personal art gallery for 32 years.

Matt Busby
1909–1994
Football Manager

Early life and playing career Matt Busby was born into a mining family in Bellshill in 1909. His father was killed in the First World War, but despite the financial strain this placed on his family he managed to escape working in the mines – the normal lot of his peers – through his footballing talents. He signed for a junior side, transferring to Manchester City in 1928 and Liverpool in 1936.

Managerial career But it was with City's rivals, Manchester United, that he gained fame. He became manager in 1945, and the club won FA Cup in 1948 followed by the league championship. Under Busby's leadership, Manchester United finished either first or second in the English First Division 11 times.

Tragedy at Munich He was a strong advocate of European football in the 1950s when British clubs were generally reluctant to compete on the Continent. He took the gamble of rebuilding his team in 1958, and the exciting, invigorating style of play of the young side, nicknamed the 'Busby Babes', seemed likely to bring the European Cup to Britain for the first time. But tragically, when the team was returning from a tie in Belgrade, their plane was involved in a crash after a stop at Munich Airport. Eight of the side, as well as other team officials, journalists and air crew, were killed; Busby himself was severely injured, and hourly bulletins had to be issued to inform a shocked nation of his state of health.

Success in '68 To Busby's credit, he patiently reconstructed the side until European Cup success came in 1968 when Manchester United became the first English club to win the trophy. Yet despite his success, Busby was always revered even more for his gentlemanly demeanour and quiet dignity. In 1969 he relinquished the managerial post he had held for 24 years, and he stayed a director and influential figure at the club until his death.

Henry Campbell-Bannerman
1836–1908
Prime Minister

Family background Henry was the second of three children of James Campbell, a prominent Glasgow draper who became Lord Provost of the city. He added the name Bannerman in 1872 in accordance with the terms of the will of his maternal uncle, who left him a large amount of money. The child of a Conservative-supporting family – both his father and his brother were Tories – he became a supporter of liberal politics while at university. He studied at both Glasgow and Cambridge until 1861, when he returned to join his father's business as a partner. At the second attempt, he was elected MP for Stirling in 1868.

Political career Campbell-Bannerman moved steadily through a succession of junior posts in Gladstone's administrations, including the challenging chief secretaryship for Ireland, a job which was a graveyard for the aspirations of ambitious politicians. Charles Stewart Parnell said of him, 'as an Irish secretary he left things alone – a sensible thing for an Irish secretary'. He was Secretary for War in 1886 and 1892–95, and emerged as party leader in 1899. He became Prime Minister in 1905 and steered the Liberal Party to its famous landslide victory in the 1906 general election.

Irish Home Rule and struggles with the Lords A major contemporary political preoccupation was the granting of Home Rule to Ireland. Campbell-Bannerman was vociferous in his support for Irish devolution, and was active in drawing up the second Home Rule bill in 1892, which passed the Commons but was thrown out of the Lords. This was not the last of his public skirmishes with the second chamber: during his brief time as premier he saw the Lords bitterly oppose his three main reforming proposals – an extension of the rights of trades unions, the disallowing of more than one vote per voter, and a reform of education. Only the first of these survived to become law. Campbell-Bannerman expressed his anger at the Lords' thwarting the will of the electors and, although he did not live to see it, the plans he laid for curbing the the unelected house's power were ultimately manifested in the 1911 Parliament Act.

Peacemaking in South Africa

He was a focus for opposition to the Boer War (1899–1902) and was highly critical of the conduct of the war by the Government, especially of the destruction of the Boers' farms and the moving of their people into concentration camps. He also stopped the importation into the Transvaal of Chinese slave labour and encouraged a policy of reconciliation to the two defeated republics, with the introduction of representative assemblies.

His talents Campbell-Bannerman's administration was responsible for the introduction of the old age pension. He was also a fervent supporter of women's suffrage. He always remained on the radical wing of his party and was among the first to recognise the talents of Lloyd George, whom he promoted in the face of opposition from those who resented the Welshman's humble background. A patient and popular man renowned for his sense of humour, Campbell-Bannerman was one of the last of the great Liberal prime ministers, with the classic Liberal commitments to free trade, democracy and reconciliation.

Thomas Carlyle
1795–1881
Essayist and historian

Rigorous early life Thomas Carlyle was born in Ecclefechan, the son of a stonemason-turned-farmer. He received a rigidly Calvinist upbringing, and its moral lessons continued to influence him long after his adolescent loss of faith. In 1809 he walked the whole 100 miles from his Borders home to Edinburgh, where he studied at the university until 1813. After graduating he intended to study first for the ministry, then for the law, spending the intervening time teaching, for which his irritable and sarcastic temperament made him singularly ill-equipped.

Early writing career Carlyle began writing by about 1818, and throughout the 1820s he made money by translating from German, especially the works of Goethe, as well as from journalism. However, he did not obtain regular work, and money was scarce during this time.

Marriage to Jane Welsh In 1826 Carlyle married Jane Welsh, an intelligent and unusual individual. Theirs was a quarrelsome, unsatisfactory relationship, but they appear to have been genuinely fond of one another, although Jane was said later to have declared that she had married 'for ambition', and was miserable. The couple remained childless, and Jane complained about the lack of attention she received from her husband, who required utter solace when writing and was prone to fits of depression. But neither of them was easy to live with; Samuel Butler was to remark, 'It was very good of God to let Carlyle and Mrs Carlyle marry one another and so make only two people miserable instead of four, besides being very amusing.'

Fame in London In 1834 the Carlyles moved to London where they took up residence at 5 Cheyne Row in Chelsea. Here they gathered around them a new circle of friends who included the foremost literary and intellectual talents of the day. They were great conversation-alists, although Carlyle's chronic indigestion and his sarcastic and dogmatic nature tended to make him a difficult dinner host and guest.

Literary output

The London move proved to be a time-ly one for his writing; in 1834 Carlyle began work on the book which was to bring him major success, *The French Revolution*. It was not pub-lished until 1837, however; he had lent the manuscript to the philosopher John Stuart Mill to read, and Mill's maid had acci-dentally thrown it on the fire while tidying, resulting in a loss of five months' work. *On Heroes and Hero Worship*, *Chartism*, *Past and Present*, *Cromwell's Letters and Speeches* and *Frederick the Great* all followed over the next two decades, outlining Carlyle's dissat-isfaction with and disapproval of modern society, and his belief in the cult of a great man or benign autocrat as political and moral leader of a nation.

While the experience of the 20th century makes it impossible to accept much of what Carlyle espoused, his work is worth reading for the originality and power of the writing alone.

Andrew Carnegie
1835–1919
American industrialist and philanthropist

Poverty of early life Andrew Carnegie's life story is a classic one of
the poor-boy-made-good. He was born in 1835, the elder son of
a Dunfermline linen weaver. Like many others, the family was
hard hit by the depression in 1848, and emigrated to the USA to
join a relative already in Pennsylvania.

Realisation of the American dream Andrew gained work first in
a textile mill, then as a telegraphist, and finally joined the
Pennsylvania Railroad Company as a clerk in 1853. Over the following decade, by a combination of talent, luck and ruthlessness,
he worked his way up to a top position in the company. He was
one of the first to see and exploit the importance of the railway
sleeping car, and he used his contacts in and knowledge of the railways to buy stock at low prices, later selling for vast amounts. He
was a millionaire by the time he was 30.

Consolidation of his power His railway interests naturally led to
investment in the iron industry, and the Civil War (1861–65)
gave him a great opportunity, with the expansion of the railways
and the need to replace wooden bridges with iron for the carrying
of Union troops and supplies. He invested in oil wells, and in
1867 he started one of the first steelworks in America. By the
1880s he was the undisputed leader of the American iron and steel
industry. His wealth was not achieved without cost; a strike at one
of his steelmills during the depression of 1892 was put down with
great severity and damage to his public image.

Conversion to philanthropy By 1900 Carnegie had decided that
he must stop earning money and start spending it in ways which
would benefit others: 'The man who dies ... rich dies disgraced',
he stated. His most famous bequests were for a chain of over 2500
public libraries throughout Britain and North America; a man

without formal education, he himself had appreciated the value of access to a library when he was a telegraphist. Multitudinous other trusts and endowments were set up; the four ancient Scottish universities also benefitted, as did his home town of Dunfermline.

Love of Scotland and Skibo Carnegie never lost his love of Scotland, and at the turn of the century he bought the 30,000-acre Skibo estate in Sutherland where he built a castle. He entertained royals, nobles and the famous, living apparently in the style of a Highland noble, with his guests being piped in to dinner each evening. But the castle was also adopted to 20th-century living, and was fitted with the latest modern conveniences and luxuries, such as a bath which, at the flick of a switch, would rotate on a turntable from an adjoining bathroom into his bedroom. Carnegie delighted in demonstrating this to his guests – with one demonstration unfortunately taking place while his wife was still in the bath. Other features around the castle were adapted to take account of his tiny stature – he never grew to more than 5 feet 1 inch in height.

Personal life Throughout his life Carnegie had been much under the influence of his mother. Only after she died did he marry, in 1887; he was over 60 when his only daughter was born. He himself died in Massachussetts at the age of 84, having given away over $350 million in his lifetime.

Celtic FC team of 1966–67
First British side to win the European Cup

History Founded in 1888 by a group of Glasgow Irish to raise money to alleviate the dreadful poverty of the city's East End, Celtic FC rose to become one of world football's giants. Success, controversy, disappointment and tragedy all peppered the club's history but their finest footballing year was in 1966–67, when they won every competition they entered: Glasgow Cup, League Cup, League championship, Scottish Cup and European Cup.

Style of play Celebrated for their joyous, attacking, imaginative football, this side had, remarkably, no weak links and several truly world-class individuals. But what makes that Celtic team worth remembering is not only the fact that they won, but how they won. A quote from their manager, Jock **Stein**, before the European Cup final best illustrates their remarkable philosophy: 'If it should happen that we lose to Inter Milan, we want to be remembered … for the football we played. We want to make neutrals everywhere glad that we qualified.' Celtic's all-Scottish side won the match 2–1.

Achievement Stein was well aware of his own talents and those of his team. He was also aware that jealousy from outside the country, and the vile sectarianism which continues to infect and corrupt the game in Scotland, would make some attempt to belittle their achievement. This was reflected in his famous quote about the team: 'The fact that a Scottish side had become the first British winners of the European Cup was a marvellous thing for us. It was Celtic's day and nothing could take that away from us.' After their crowning moment in Lisbon, the great Liverpool manager, Bill Shankly, pushed his way into the dressing room to hail Stein with the words, 'John, you're immortal!' Shankly's prophetic judgement is applicable not only to Stein but to that Celtic team, the finest club side Scotland has ever produced.

Thomas Chalmers
1780–1847
Founder of the Free Church of Scotland

Thomas Chalmers was the most famous and dynamic minister of his day, a vociferous advocate of social and religious reform and the leader of the party who walked out of the General Assembly of the Church of Scotland in 1843, sensationally splitting the Church in two. Yet despite his contemporary achievements, his name is not widely known today, and this is possibly an indicator of how much of his time, and how essentially unradical, he was.

Early trials and mission The sixth of 14 children of an Anstruther merchant family, Thomas entered St Andrew's University at 11 years of age. His first appointment came as minister of Kilmany in 1803. He had come close to losing his faith while he was a student, and in 1810 he experienced a deep religious crisis from which he emerged an evangelical with a desire to proselytise and convert. His preaching, already well known, was enhanced by new qualities of independence of thought, persuasiveness and enthusiasm, and he remained one of the foremost orators of his day.

Religious work in society By the end of 1814 he was given an important ministry, at the Tron Church on the fringes of Glasgow's recently industrialised East End. Poor relief was failing many people in need in the area, and what Chalmers called 'home heathenism' was rife. He put into practice one of his central beliefs, that the church's spiritual role must go hand-in-hand with the social, and the importance of self-help and self-reliance. He established a network of workers, including elders and deacons, and started schools. His ideas were not radical: they took as their framework the established order, and depended largely for impact on reforming zeal, personal commitment and the appeal of the new. But his work in Glasgow at that time was a great success: charity dependence lessened, drunkenness decreased and parents

47

took more responsibility for their children. He repeated his success at St John's in Glasgow from 1820 until 1823, when he took the chair of moral philosophy at St Andrews. In 1828 he became professor of theology at Edinburgh University, a post which brought him into direct contact with wider church issues.

The Disruption of 1843 Throughout the 1830s the Church's General Assembly, its governing body, was preoccupied with the question of who appointed ministers – congregations or local landowners. For the evangelical party it was unacceptable that the landowners' powers of patronage should be brought to bear in a ministerial appointment. A compromise reached in 1833 was overturned by the civil courts five years later. Matters came to a head in the General Assembly of 1843, when Chalmers led 470 ministers – a third of the total number – out of the hall and the Church, taking a fifth of the congregations with them. For Chalmers, who believed in an established church, this was a hard step to take, and it was one which split the country. His work with the urban poor, now with a much narrower base to operate from, was severely undermined. The success which the new Free Church of Scotland achieved in the last four years of Chalmers' life was due largely to his skills and ideals, but the new church found its success difficult to sustain without the dynamism of its first leader.

Prince Charles Edward Stuart, 'Bonnie Prince Charlie'
1720–1788
de jure King Charles III

Early life Charles was born in Rome on 31 December 1720, the elder son of the titular King James VIII. He was an intelligent child, able to speak English, French and Italian despite a sporadic education. But his preference was always for active rather than scholarly pursuits, and he took part enthusiastically in military engagements on the Continent.

Start of the Rising Charles became the centre of hopes of a Stuart restoration and was seen by the French government as an important pawn in their constantly shifting power game with Britain. A promised French invasion of England in 1744 never materialised through a combination of bad weather and the ships of the Royal Navy in the English Channel. But Charles was determined that his time had come, and he set sail for Scotland in the summer of 1745, landing in the Hebrides with only seven men. He was welcomed by several of the Highland chiefs, but they had little enthusiasm for a rising without other aid. The prince had charm and courage, however; when the chiefs told him that he should go home, he replied, 'I am come home,' and by the time he raised his standard at Glenfinnan on 19 August, 600 men had already joined him.

Stunning early successes The ever-growing army marched south through Perth, where they were joined by Charles' great general, Lord George **Murray**, and on to Edinburgh. The capital surrendered on 17 September, with only the castle holding out, and Charles held court at Holyrood Palace. The Jacobites' crushing victory at the battle of Prestonpans on 21 September alarmed the Government in London for the first time, and troops were hastily recalled from the Continent. On 1 November Charles' army marched out of the capital headed for London. Carlisle fell on 8 November and under Murray's guidance the Jacobite forces outmanoeuvred two Government armies, under Wade and Cumberland, to arrive at Derby at the start of December.

Disillusionment, retreat and Culloden By now, however, the chiefs were increasingly nervous at their own isolation; their men, now far from their undefended home lands, had begun deserting; the promised back-up of French troops had not materialised; and the English Jacobites had not risen. But what the chiefs were unaware of was the panic which was spreading through London, where George II, with bags hurriedly packed, was preparing to return to Hanover. In this light it is irresistible to speculate about what might have been had Charles' plan, of making a dash for London, prevailed. However, despite his arguments and pleas, the will of the chiefs prevailed, and the Jacobite army turned north on 6 December, skillfully outmanoeuvring the Government forces again, and then defeating them at Falkirk on 17 January. But the army of the Duke of Cumberland caught up with them at Culloden in April of 1746, where Charles, despite desertion and fatigue among his men and against Murray's advice, chose to fight. The Jacobites were decimated.

Fugitive Culloden marked the end of hopes of a restoration of the Stuart monarchy. Charles spent the next five months a fugitive in the Highlands and islands with a price of £30,000 on his head. He escaped on a French ship in September, having been helped by many, including Flora **Macdonald**. The Highlands were punished terribly by the British Government, who systematically set out to dismantle the social and cultural fabric of Scottish Gaeldom.

Failure For a man who had devoted his entire life to one cause, to experience its shattering was unbearable, and Charles' personality crumbled under the dreadful weight of the failure. He spent the rest of his life in France and, latterly, in Italy, sinking into alcoholism, ill-treating his Scottish mistress, Clementina Walkinshaw, then his wife, Princess Louisa of Stolberg, during their disastrous marriage. He continued to hope for a Stuart restoration, and made secret trips to London in the 1750s to try to revive flagging Jacobite hopes. However, his own disintegration from dashing youth into shambling middle age meant that, when he became the head of the Jacobite cause on his father's death in 1766, his restoration as king of Scotland, England and Ireland seemed further off than ever. Charles had one child, Charlotte, by his mistress Clementina, and she lived with her father from 1780. She was his only comfort in old age, and he loved her deeply, creating her Duchess of Albany.

Charles was always racked by guilt over the fate which had befallen his men in the Forty-five and the vicious punishments subsequently meted out in the Highlands by the Government in London. When he died at Rome on 31 January 1788, a lone piper played the lament *Lochaber No More* in the courtyard outside his room.

Hugh Clapperton
1788–1827
Explorer

Youth   Hugh Clapperton's life is a classic tale of 19th-century exploration and adventure. At 13 years of age he became a cabin boy on a ship sailing the Atlantic from Liverpool, and even at this early age he was said to have shown spirit by refusing to black the captain's boots.

Adventures in North America   Hugh joined the navy, eventually reaching the rank of captain, and served in the East Indies from 1808 to 1814, and then in Canada. He was popular as well as personally courageous: while in Canada his attempt to save the life of a boy on a journey across the ice cost him the use of a hand. He was adopted by Indians at this time, hunting with them and almost marrying a Huron princess.

African exploration   After returning to Scotland in 1817 he became interested in African exploration, and was part of a group which set out from Britain in 1822 to look for the source of the Niger. They travelled across the Sahara via Lake Chad to Sokoto, and were only a few days from their goal, but the local sultan would not let them progress. They were forced to return to Britain in 1825. He was part of another expedition which left at the end of that year, but disease struck almost as soon as they set foot in Africa, and a feverish Clapperton had physically to carry his dysentery-stricken servant. The party finally reached Sokoto, where they were detained once more. Here Clapperton was wooed by a rich widow who, taken by his tall physique and good looks, followed him on horseback, dressed in scarlet and gold robes and serenading him with bands of musicians. But Clapperton's health was broken with dysentery, and he died in Sokoto, his spirit broken by the failure to reach his goal.

Jim Clark
1936–1968
World champion racing driver

Family background Born into a Fife farming family, Jim Clark was educated in Edinburgh. His family moved to Berwickshire, and Jim left school at 16 to work on their sheep farm.

First interest His interest in motor racing was first sparked by the local motor club, where he took part in events, winning his first race at the age of 20. He became Scottish Speed Champion in the following two years, and at 22 became the first post-war driver to lap a British circuit at over 100 mph. Clark worked his way through the racing circuits until, in 1960, he joined the Lotus team, taking part in Formula 1 and Formula 2 racing.

Early crash In 1961 there was a foreshadowing of the disaster that was to come for Clark when, at the Monza track, he collided with a fellow-racer, who was killed along with 14 spectators.

Achievements In 1963, after almost succeeding the previous year, he became world champion with seven Grand Prix wins. He repeated his success in 1965, taking the chequered flag in five races in a row. In that year he also became the first non-American for almost 50 years to win the Indianapolis 500.

Final tragedy Trouble with his car in the 1966 and '67 championships caused a temporary fall-off in form, but in spite of this he now enjoyed a record-breaking 25 wins in Grand Prix races. A return to form seemed sure to bring victory in the 1968 championship, but while practising for a race at Hockenheim in April his car went off a bend at 120 mph, killing him instantly. The cause of the crash was never identified.

Clark had already been hailed as one of the finest racing drivers the world had seen. In 1965 he was honoured by his home town of Duns by being made its first honourary burgess, and the Jim Clark Memorial room in the town displays many of his trophies.

Thomas Cochrane
1775–1860
Naval commander

Family background and personality   The name of Thomas Cochrane was as familiar to his contemporaries as that of Nelson, yet today is almost forgotten. Born in Lanarkshire, he was marked out for a naval career by his family from infancy, and he served first under his uncle, a captain, before being given his own command. He was never renowned as a tactician, but his daring and bravery were legendary: in 1801, during the Napoleonic Wars, he came ashore to attend a fancy-dress ball full of French officers in Valetta, dressed as a British seaman, while his ship was preying on French and Spanish vessels in the surrounding area.

His framing, public disgrace and rehabilitation   Cochrane's forthrightness and lack of political caution repeatedly brought him into conflict with the naval authorities. After his election to Parliament and a personal campaign against naval abuses he was implicated in a charge of fraud, and although he maintained his innocence, he was imprisoned for a year and fined. This public disgrace apparently finished his career, and from 1818 to 1828 he was engaged as head of the navies of Chile – helping the country win independence from Spain – Brazil and Greece. But in 1831 he succeeded his father as Earl of Dundonald, and the following year his rehabilitation in Britain was marked by a free pardon and restoration to the navy as rear admiral.

Marriage   In 1812, on learning that his uncle was planning to marry him off to an heiress, Cochrane hurriedly wed his sweetheart, Katherine, at Gretna. It was a move he never regretted, always considering his wife 'a rich equivalent' for the loss of a fortune. Throughout his varied life he was also a keen inventor, and was among the first to commend the benefits of steam power and screw propellers to the navy.

Lord Cockburn
1779–1854
Judge

Political background Henry Cockburn was born on 26 October 1779 in Parliament Close, Edinburgh. The child of a prominent Tory family, he abandoned his political inheritance while studying law at Edinburgh University and became a Whig. It was a commitment from which he never wavered, although it would later cost him advancement in his career.

Legal career Cockburn became an advocate in 1800 and gained success as counsel for the defence in criminal cases, in which his broad Scottish accent and his turn of phrase combined with his sincerity and sympathetic demeanour to sway juries to return unexpected not-guilty verdicts. One of those he defended was an associate of **Burke & Hare**; during the trial Cockburn was said to have remarked, 'except that he murdered, Burke was a gentlemanly fellow'. Cockburn was made Solicitor General for Scotland in 1830 after the Whig Government came to power, and was influential in drawing up the Scottish Reform Bill, extending the franchise. In 1834 he became a judge at the Court of Session.

His writings Cockburn's fame has survived largely due to the posthumous publication of his journals, mainly in *Memorials of his Time*, covering the period 1779 to 1830, and *Circuit Journeys*, dealing with 1837 to 1854. These works catalogue not only the social upheavals and great uncertainty which swept across Scotland in the aftermath of the French Revolution, over the Reform Bill and throughout the early Victorian era, but record in a human and witty style the characters and manners of contemporary Edinburgh society. **Stevenson** sent from Samoa for a copy of *Memorials* for its portrait of **Braxfield**, on which he drew for *Weir of Hermiston*.

William Collins
1789–1853
Publisher

Early life William Collins was born in Eastwood in 1789. He left school at 11 years of age to work at the loom, and 17 or 18 years had become a clerk at Pollokshaws mill.

Publishing ventures and motives He was a devout Christian and started up a Sunday school in the mill, offering religious instruction to his colleagues. From this he moved on to holding classes in arithmetic and English on week nights. In 1813 Collins opened a school for the children of the Glasgow poor. It was shortly after this that the evangelical minister Thomas **Chalmers** began his ministry in the city, and Collins was much influenced by his ideas. By 1819 Collins had decided that the best way to ensure the spread of Christianity was through publishing and bookselling rather than teaching, and he went into partnership with Chalmers' brother, Charles. Two-thirds of the books sold in Scotland at this time were religious, and this was reflected in Collins' list. He did not forget his first profession, however, and published his first schoolbook in 1821.

Beliefs and personal life Religious belief was an ever-present in Collins' personal and professional life. He was a friend of the anti-slave-trade campaigner, William Wilberforce, and displayed an abolitionist petition in his bookshop. He travelled extensively throughout Scotland, speaking on a temperance platform. Commercial success and religious commitment masked personal tragedy, however; as with so many families at this time, all but one of his children died before him.

Business success By the 1840s the Collins firm was well established; its list included a dictionary and the Bible. A London branch had been opened by his surviving son, also William, who consolidated the firm's commercial success later in the century.

St Columba
521–597
Missionary to Scotland

Early life in Ireland Columba was born in Donegal into an Irish chiefly family. As a youth he studied scripture under St Finnian at Clonard, and even then he already had a reputation as a worker of miracles. By the time he left Ireland he had founded several monasteries, including that at Derry in 546 and Durrow in 553.

Exile to Scotland Columba was no milk-and-water saint, however; after a violation of sanctuary by the king of Ireland in 561 Columba called out his warrior family against him, and is believed to have taken part personally in the ensuing battle at Cuildremhne, in which he received a wound which stayed with him as a livid scar down his left side. He was censured for his belligerence, although his punishment is not known, and missionary exile may have been a voluntary penance. In 561 he set sail with 12 followers. His coracle was washed ashore on Iona in the Hebrides, and it was there he built his monastery.

His achievements in Scotland The Romans had left a Christian legacy in the southern half of Scotland on which Columba built, but the northern Picts were still pagan, and he set out to convert them. His monastery became a missionary school and he founded many churches on the mainland and in the Hebrides. Columba's piety was renowned, although he spent most of his life on Iona in religious observance, manual toil and writing; he is believed to have transcribed 300 books. The atmosphere of peace on Columba's windswept island was still discernable centuries later; after his visit there Dr Johnson said 'that man is little to be envied ... whose piety would not grow warmer among the ruins of Iona'. The bodies of several Scottish kings and leaders have been buried on Columba's island, and the abbey itself was restored under the guidance of George **MacLeod**.

Sean Connery
Born 1930
Actor

Varied early career Thomas Connery was born in Edinburgh in 1930 and left school at 13. He drifted through a multitude of different jobs from coffin polisher, bricklayer and milkman to bodybuilder and swimming-trunks model, before he gained a place in the chorus of a production of the musical *South Pacific* in London's West End in 1951. He worked steadily in minor roles on stage and in film and television throughout the 1950s.

Fame as 007 Connery's first big break came when he was cast as secret agent James Bond in *Dr No* (1962). He was apparently chosen over other, more famous actors – such as Richard Burton and Roger Moore – because he was initially paid only £15,000, as opposed to the $1 million which an established star might then have cost. Connery became closely identified with the part of suave and debonair secret agent over the next decade, although he continued to appear in other films, such as *Marnie* and *The Man who Would be King*.

Awards and personality Since leaving his role as Bond Connery has diversified into a greater range of parts, winning a BAFTA Best Actor award for his part in *The Name of the Rose*, and an Oscar for *The Untouchables* in 1987. He was also voted The World's Sexiest Man in recent years. Connery is a fine character actor who today can command up to $10 million per film and is probably the world's most famous living Scot, yet he remains relatively unaffected by his fame: according to one film director, 'With the exception of Lassie, he's the only person I know who's never been spoiled by success.'

Billy Connolly
Born 1942
Entertainer

Style and influence Billy Connolly has been the most successful and popular all-round entertainer to emerge from Scotland in recent years. His humour, the centrepiece of his success and his talent, is wide in its appeal, with observations on the ironies of life complemented by a hilarious line in Rabelaisian and lavatorial humour. Although his background, like many of his contemporaries, was in the Scottish folk-music scene, he can be seen in many ways as the forerunner of the new type of comic that emerged in Britain in the 1980s.

Background on the folk scene Originally a welder in the Clyde shipyards, he became a professional musician in 1965, appearing with Gerry Rafferty and Tam Harvey in The Humblebums folk group before going solo. He worked in clubs around the country with an act which, initially, was mainly music with a scattering of jokes and comic observations. The balance of the content gradually changed, with the observations developing into longer monologues and assuming greater importance.

Fame and success From the early 1970s Connolly's name was becoming more well-known throughout Scotland, and his first break came shortly afterwards, with appearances on TV chat shows and with the satirical single *D.I.V.O.R.C.E.* Connolly's success in his comedy act has been consolidated by his acting, which has ranged from appearances in dramas like *Just Another Saturday* in 1975 through film work to more recent roles in American sitcoms *Head of the Class* and *Billy*. Despite his worldwide fame he remains a pleasant, affable man with a reassuringly common-sense attitude to his talents and success.

James Connolly
1868–1916
Socialist and Irish rebel leader

Achievements Born into a poor Irish Catholic family in the Cowgate in Edinburgh, James left school to work at the age of 11. Despite this unpromising start he educated himself, going on to become one the most original and influential socialist thinkers of his day and one of the few left-wing theoreticians ever to rise from the working class.

Work and beliefs He is believed to have joined the British army at 14 by falsifying his age, and was stationed in Dublin where he later met his wife, Lillie, a Protestant from Co. Wicklow. In 1890 he returned to Edinburgh to organise the city's working-class socialist movement, but by 1896 he was back in Ireland, lecturing and promoting socialist causes there as well as in the US and Scotland. Connolly linked his personal ideals of socialism and Irish nationalism, and asserted in *Labour, Nationality and Religion* the right of Catholics to be socialists, at a time when there was great hostility to the movement in the Church.

Rebellion and death In 1916 Connolly, now an influential union leader, vehemently anti-war, and newly appointed commander of the Irish Citizen Army, was persuaded to join in the Easter Rising of 1916 against British rule in Ireland. The rising was suppressed by the British Government and its leaders executed, the wounded Connolly being tied to a chair to be shot by firing squad.

Legacies in Ireland and Scotland Ironically, despite Connolly's attempts to introduce a socialist dimension to Irish politics and nationalism, his execution resulted in his absorption into the pantheon of mainstream Irish nationalism, with little attention being paid in Ireland to his other thought. His fame as a socialist remained in Scotland, however, where John **Maclean** was among those influenced by his ideas.

Kate Cranston

1850–1934
Tearoom owner and patron of the arts

Family influences Kate Cranston was born in Glasgow into an entrepreneurial family; her father was a hotelier and tea dealer, and other relatives were also in business. Unusually, there were also vigorous, educated, entrepreneurial women in the family – one of her cousins owned and managed a hotel.

The Glasgow tearooms The new tearooms which appeared in Glasgow in the second half of the 19th century were fostered in large part by the desire to promote temperance in a city sensitive to the coupling of the twin vices of drink and poverty. The social constraints which kept women at home were also loosening, and the tearooms in which they could meet demonstrated the city's prosperity and its outgoing nature. Kate's brother, Stuart, had opened a tearoom, but it was against her family's wishes that she followed suit in 1878. There were to be four Miss Cranston's Tearooms around the city centre – in Argyle St, Buchanan St, Ingram St and, most famously, Sauchiehall St – and she also provided the tearooms for Glasgow's International Exhibitions in 1901 and 1911. She ran her tearooms with the precision of a drill sergeant and standards were never less than impeccable.

Style and artistic patronage Although she was one of many tearoom owners, she was undoubtedly the most famous, a feat achieved by her eccentric appearance, reminiscent of Queen Victoria (she continued to wear mid-Victorian crinolines long after they had gone out of fashion, coupled with flouncy hats), her astute business sense (she received the accolade of appearing in the 'Men You Know' column of the Glasgow magazine, *The Bailie*) and her fostering of avant-garde artistic talents in the design of her establishments. She introduced Glaswegians to the work of **Mackintosh** and Margaret Macdonald who, along with George

61

Walton, designed the interiors, fittings and furnishings for most of her tearooms. Miss Cranston's association with Mackintosh reached its apogee in the Willow Tearooms in Sauchiehall St, where customers sat on, at and among works of art which would now collectively fetch millions of pounds. (Part of these tearooms have now been restored.) The unique nature of the Cranston tearooms was summed up by artist Muirhead Bone during the 1920s: 'Those Glasgow tea-rooms were things of extraordinary beauty and originality, and one cannot find any restaurants in London today to compare with them.'

Later years In 1892 Kate had married John Cochrane, eight years younger than herself and the owner of an engineering works. Theirs was a close and happy marriage, and Kate was devastated by his death at a relatively early age in 1917. Although she had run her business on her own she now lost the will to continue, and sold off her tearooms and her Mackintosh-designed house to live in a hotel. She dressed in black for the rest of her life. On her death in 1934, a third of her estate went to her niece and the remainder to the poor of the city.

James Crichton
1560–1585
Prodigy

Dazzling accomplishments   James, the renowned 'Admirable Crichton', was the son of Robert Crichton, the Lord Advocate. He attended St Andrews University from the age of 10, where George **Buchanan** was one of his tutors. He graduated in 1575, by which time he was said to have been master of ten languages. He was also handsome, a superb horseman and fencer, and accomplished in all social graces.

Successes in Europe   In 1577 he arrived in Paris, where he challenged professors of the city to pose him questions on any subject in any of his languages, and proceeded to acquit himself brilliantly before masters and students. To round things off, he won a public joust at the Louvre next day. He is believed to have joined the French army, and for once he did not fare well, as he is recorded as arriving destitute in Genoa the following year. However, he repeated his Parisian intellectual display there, and again in Venice the following year.

Death in a jealous street brawl   In 1582 he was engaged by the Duke of Mantua to be tutor to his son, Vincenzo, a youth of fierce temper. Given Crichton's talents and his predilection for displaying them publicly, it is perhaps not surprising that the two did not get on. Crichton was ambushed returning from his lover's house one night, and although he saw off several of his assailants, he dropped his guard on discovering that his pupil was among the gang, whereupon Vincenzo stabbed Crichton in the heart.

The Admirable Crichton has become synonymous with complete accomplishment, and **Barrie** used the name in his 1902 play about the perfect butler.

A. J. Cronin
1896–1981
Writer

Early years, war service and marriage Archibald Joseph Cronin was born in Cardross, but moved to Dumbarton at the age of seven to live with his mother's family after the death of his father. He studied medicine at Glasgow University, breaking off from his course to join the Royal Naval Volunteer Reserve as a surgeon during the First World War. He qualified in 1919, and married a fellow doctor two years later.

Short medical career Cronin's medical career was short: his first practice was in a Welsh mining valley, and he later became Medical Inspector of Mines for two years until 1926, when he went into private practice in London. He was forced to stop working when his health failed in 1930.

Dr Finlay **and other works** It was while recuperating on a farm near Inveraray that Cronin wrote in three months his first book, the brooding *Hatter's Castle*, a work in the style of George Douglas Brown's influential *The House with the Green Shutters*. The book's instant success both at home and abroad allowed Cronin to abandon completely his medical practice and to write full time. He produced many famous works over the following decades, including *The Citadel* and *Keys of the Kingdom*. His writing was closely based on real life and individuals, set in situations posing moral dilemmas. His popularity was sustained by radio and TV adaptations of stories from his Scots novels of his own experiences as a doctor, *Dr Finlay's Casebook*.

Cronin worked for the Ministry of Information during the Second World War, and was based in the US. In later life he settled in Switzerland.

Alexander Cruden
1701–1770
Scholar, religious preacher and eccentric

Early mental illness A native of Aberdeen, Alexander was educated in the city at Marischal College. He had planned to enter the ministry, but an unhappy love affair upset his mental balance so much that he was committed to an asylum for a time. From then on, his mental balance was always fragile.

Bad luck in London Cruden did not have much luck in his professional life, either: in 1722 he moved to London where he later became secretary to the Earl of Derby, a post from which he was soon dismissed for his ignorance of French pronunciation. His attempted remedy of the situation, a crash course in French taken in his new lodgings, where all the other residents were French, did not move his former employer. In 1737 an attempt to start a bookselling business failed on the death of Queen Caroline, patron of Cruden's famous and expensively produced bible concordance. During this time his mental condition was unstable; he escaped one period of confinement in an asylum by sawing through the bedstead to which he was chained.

Career as moral guardian After this failure he became a proofreader, assuming the name of 'Alexander the Corrector'. However, his correction also extended to the nation's morals, a task for which he believed he was ordained by heaven, with his success prophesied. From 1755 onwards he travelled the country, reproving Sabbath-breaking and profanity. He was also a prolific pamphleteer, publishing accounts of his confinements and his beliefs. Despite his eccentricities and odd behaviour, he was a sympathetic and well-liked character, and gained fame for the quality of his biblical scholarship.

R. B. Cunninghame Graham
1852–1936
Traveller, writer, socialist and nationalist

Robert Bontine Cunninghame Graham is the last in a series of larger-than-life characters who appear throughout Scottish history. He was a brilliant figure who excelled at whatever he turned his hand to, but who never settled at one thing for long.

Early life and South American influences   He was born in London, of an unusual family: his father's family, lairds of Gartmore, could trace descent from King Robert II, while his maternal grandmother was a Spanish noblewoman. She played a large part in his upbringing: Spanish was the first language he learned; he was taught to ride in the Spanish way; and he spent long periods in South America, riding with the gauchos and travelling. He was held in such esteem there that a city in Argentina was named 'Don Roberto' in his honour, after his death. In appearance, Cunninghame Graham was described by contemporaries as looking like a Spanish nobleman.

Political career as socialist and nationalist   His political career was wide-ranging: in 1886 he was elected Liberal MP for North-West Lanarkshire, but the following year he was imprisoned in Pentonville Prison for his participation in the 'Bloody Sunday' Trafalgar Square demonstration on behalf of the unemployed. He had a compassionate nature which tended to champion the underdog, and was soon converted to socialism, founding the Scottish Labour Party with Keir **Hardie**. He became its first president in 1888. During his time as an MP he visited Ireland, where he was entranced by Parnell; when the Irish statesman died in 1891 Cunninghame Graham was the only non-Irish MP to attend his funeral. In 1892 he retired from the House of Commons (in which he had gained notoriety as the first member to be suspended for using the word 'damn'). After the First World War his political interests were centred on Scotland, and he became president of the Scottish National Party in 1934.

Travel writings and personal relationships His travels in little-known lands, including Morocco and South America, are well documented, with his travel writings and his fiction having the same vivid and appealing directness. A noted wit and man of great style, he numbered among his friends some of the most famous writers and artists of his day, such as Morris, Whistler, Shaw, Wells and Beerbohm, and, more idiosyncratically, Buffalo Bill, whom he had befriended during his travels in Mexico.

In 1879 Cunninghame Graham married a Chilean poet, Gabriela de la Balmondière, whom he had met when his horse knocked her down in Paris. The couple had no children, and when she died in 1906 he dug with his own hands her grave at the ruined priory on Inchmahome Island on the Lake of Menteith. He died in Buenos Aires 30 years later, and his body was brought home to be buried next to his wife's.

David Dale
1739–1806
Industrialist and philanthropist

David Dale was a successful industrialist whose business acumen was coupled with an acute sense of social responsibility: he was among the first in Scotland to grasp the opportunities of the Industrial Revolution, and was also among the earliest enlightened industrialists.

Early commercial success   He was born on 6 January in Stewarton, the son of a local grocer. As a small child he was sent out to work herding cattle, and later served an apprenticeship with a weaver in Paisley. He continued to work in the textile trade, establishing his own lucrative linen-importing business.

His move to New Lanark   The dissolution of his business left him with healthy profits, some of which he used to buy the first cotton mill in Scotland, at Rothesay, in 1778. In 1777 he had married the daughter of a director of the Royal Bank of Scotland, and he was appointed the bank's first Glasgow agent in 1783. The following year, at a dinner in the city, he met Richard Arkwright, inventor of the mechanised spinning machine, with whom he went into partnership to set up mills at New Lanark. The association was dissolved when Arkwright suffered a setback in establishing the patent to his invention, but Dale pressed on, and spinning had begun in New Lanark by 1786.

His philanthropy in business life   The site, by the Falls of Clyde, had the necessary water to power the machines, but mill work was not popular in the area, so Dale brought in pauper children from the poorhouses of Glasgow and Edinburgh, providing them with accommodation and education. By 1795 the New Lanark mills, a model of their type, employed 1,334 workers. Dale also attempted to provide employment for those who had been cleared off the land in the Highlands, establishing mills at Oban and in

Sutherland. In 1791 he also helped the survivors of an emigrant ship headed for North America but which had been wrecked at Greenock, and provided them with work and accommodation. Dale had built up a tradition of benevolent and enlightened management, with care for his employees' welfare, and in 1799 he sold the New Lanark mills to his son-in-law, Robert Owen, whom he knew would carry on his work and methods.

His philanthropy in personal life Dale's philanthropy arose naturally out of his practical Christianity; in 1768 he helped to found a dissenting sect, the 'Old Independents', and became their leader and best-known preacher. His concerns were not confined to his own employees: in 1795 he became a director of the new Royal Infirmary at Glasgow, set up to help the sick poor. At the turn of the century, during a local famine, he bought in at his own expense shiploads of food, which was then sold at cost price to the poor of the city.

Lord Darnley
1545–1567
Second husband of Mary, Queen of Scots

Attributes Henry Stewart, Lord Darnley, was the son of the Earl of Lennox and the grandson of Margaret Tudor, daughter of Henry VII of England. With both Stewart and Tudor blood, he was a main claimant to the thrones of Scotland and England after his wife and cousin, **Mary**, Queen of Scots, and it was his awareness of this position coupled with his utter lack of political skill or personal attributes that led to his downfall and murder.

Marriage to the queen Mary found Darnley very attractive, and they were married on 29 July 1565. But despite this, the marriage was based primarily on political expediency – the queen needed a strong counterbalance to help her assert herself against her powerful half-brother, the Earl of Moray. Darnley's weakness and vanity were soon obvious, and the couple became estranged. Yet he craved power, and jealousy was the main reason for his participation in the murder in March 1566 of David Rizzio, the queen's secretary. Mary, politically isolated and alone, pretended a reconciliation, although even this was short-lived. When the couple's son, the future **James VI**, was christened at Stirling the following December, Darnley stayed sulking in his room, with plans in hand to leave the country. There was talk of a divorce, but Darnley fell ill at Glasgow in the new year, possibly with smallpox, and Mary brought him to a house at Kirk o' Field by Edinburgh to convalesce under her own attention.

Murder But on 9 February, hours after Mary left for a ball at Holyrood, the house was levelled in an explosion. Curiously, the unmarked bodies of Darnley and his servant were found in a garden 40 yards away, possibly having been murdered in an attempt to escape. The Earl of **Bothwell**, Mary's next husband, was accused of the murder and the queen, too, was suspected.

James Dewar
1842–1923
Inventor of the vacuum flask

Early life Born on 20 September 1842 in Kincardine, James Dewar was the youngest son of a vintner. His practical mind was demonstrated at an early age: at the age of 10 he contracted rheumatic fever after falling through the ice on a river near his home, and while he convalesced he turned his hand to making violins. (It was an instrument of which he remained fond, and in later life he would often relax at the end of a busy day by playing his violin, accompanied by his wife, into the early hours of the morning.)

Professional career Dewar went to Edinburgh University at the end of the 1850s, and quickly demonstrated his aptitude in chemistry and natural philosophy. He became a laboratory demonstrator to the professor, then in 1869 he was appointed lecturer in chemistry at Edinburgh's veterinary school. Six years later after a spell at Ghent he was appointed to a professorship in natural experimental philosophy at Cambridge, and in 1877 became professor at the Royal Institution in London following two years later; he held both posts until his death.

Inventions and discoveries An experimental and practical scientist, Dewar's particular speciality was in the liquefaction and freezing of gasses, particularly hydrogen and helium; these he envisaged as the key to opening up new areas of research in the sciences. During one of his experiments into the storing of liquid gasses he devised a vacuum jacket to maintain temperature. This became known as the Dewar flask, and was later marketed commercially as the Thermos flask. He was also a member of a government committee on explosives, and with a fellow member he developed cordite, the explosive propellant.

John Dewar
1856–1929
Spirit merchant and distiller

Family business The Dewar family's licensed grocery had been established by John Dewar's father, also John, in 1846. John junior, together with his brother, Thomas, turned their father's locally successful but small-time business into one of the giants of the world spirit trade.

Dewar brothers' successes John was born in Perth and served his apprenticeship in the family firm. He took over as manager in 1880 after his father's death, and was joined by his younger brother, Tommy, the following year. The brothers made a good team: John was responsible for the firm's successful administration and financing, and Tommy for marketing. Tommy gained sensational publicity for the firm by playing the bagpipes at the Brewer's Show in London in 1885, much to the disapproval of the show's organisers. John was made Lord Provost of Perth and served as Liberal MP for Inverness-shire from 1900 to 1916 when, as Lord Forteviot, he became the first of the 'whisky lords'. Tommy, too, became a peer, as Lord Dewar.

Advances in the whisky trade Dewar's was the first firm to recognise the possibilities of gaining new and lucrative markets for whisky in selling by the bottle, which could be taken home, rather than by the cask, which limited its sale to hotels, pubs and licensed premises. The company was also instrumental in finding new markets outside Scotland by abandoning the sale of the stronger-tasting malts, which needed an acquired taste, in favour of the less fiery and more accessible blends. The firm merged with rival Buchanan in 1915, and joined the giant conglomerate Distillers Company Ltd in 1925. Market lead has been maintained, as Dewar's White Label is now the best-selling Scotch whisky in the USA.

James Douglas
c. 1286–1330
Commander in the War of Independence

'Good' Sir James was also known as the Black Douglas because of his dark complexion and jet-coloured hair, although to the English this name could have been descriptive of his deeds. Gentle and courtly in his manners, in battle his imaginative boldness and bravery were astounding.

Early allegiance to Bruce His father had been one of the few men of rank to join the **Wallace** rebellion, for which Edward I of England had forfeited the family's Borders lands. James himself joined **Robert** Bruce in 1306, shortly before his coronation. With the king constantly throughout his darkest period in 1306–7, Douglas became his most trusted friend and right-hand man.

His ingenuity and daring Tales of Douglas' martial feats throughout the War of Independence make thrilling reading. His name was held in terror especially in the north of England, which he raided regularly and efficiently, extracting protection money from its hapless inhabitants. The Archbishop of York and the Bishop of Ely attempted to stop one such raid with a large and hastily gathered force at Mitton, north of York. The presence of a large number of clerics in the makeshift English band was reflected in the name given to their subsequent slaughter by Douglas' troops, the Chapter of Mitton. One of Douglas' most famous exploits took place on Palm Sunday in 1308: English soldiers, who had captured his castle, were surprised in church by Douglas and his followers, disguised as peasants. After their victory he led his men back to the castle where, after feasting, they burned the building to the ground by torching the remaining food and the wine casks, throwing the bodies of dead horses and English soldiers into the middle of the flames. The mingled smells of burning food, sizzling fat and human flesh were said to permeate the air for miles

around. Not surprisingly, it became known as Douglas' Larder. On another occasion, with a group of less than 100 men, he attacked and routed in Jedburgh Forest an English force 10,000-strong under Sir Thomas Richmond, carving a way through the enemy's ranks to snatch Richmond's cap from his head, then melting back into the forest again.

Bannockburn Douglas was in charge of the left wing of the Scots army at Bannockburn. He was knighted by Robert the night before the battle, and after it chased the English king and his 500-strong retinue as far as Dunbar, with a force of only 60 men. King Edward managed to escape by sea with only minutes to spare.

Death in Spain Douglas' devotion to the king was steadfast, and after Robert's death, in accordance with his wishes, he took the king's heart on crusade, making for the Holy Land. En route, Douglas and his knights were diverted into helping the king of Castile fight the Moors in Andalucía, and Douglas was killed in battle there in August 1330.

Arthur Conan Doyle
1859–1930
Writer

Background Arthur Conan Doyle was born in Edinburgh, the child of an Irish Catholic family. He graduated in medicine from Edinburgh University in 1881 but writing was his first love, and it was while working as a doctor that he invented Sherlock Holmes, his most extraordinary and enduring character.

Sherlock Holmes The cerebral Holmes and his revolutionary scientific methods of deduction were said to have been based on Joseph Bell, an eminent Edinburgh surgeon under whom Conan Doyle may have studied. He first appeared in the novel *A Study in Scarlet*, in 1887. By 1891 Conan Doyle was sufficiently sure of an income from writing to give up his medical practice. Holmes and his congenial partner, Dr John Watson, appeared over the next two years in short-story form in the *Strand Magazine*. Conan Doyle came to tire of Holmes, however, and tried to kill him off in 1893, only to have to resurrect him by popular demand a decade later in *The Return of Sherlock Holmes*.

Public profile Conan Doyle volunteered for military medical service in the Boer War (1899–1902) and wrote a defence of the British side, for which he received a knighthood. From 1909 until 1928 he helped publicise the case of Oscar Slater, a German Jew falsely accused and convicted of murder in a case which was one of Scotland's most infamous miscarriages of justice. Thanks in part to Conan Doyle's intervention the death sentence was commuted and Slater was finally released after 19 years in prison.

Other writings As well as the Sherlock Holmes stories, much of Conan Doyle's work remains in print today, a credit to his natural, flowing style and wide range of characters and interests, such as boxing, seafaring, the fantastic and spiritualism, to which he converted after his son was killed in the First World War.

William Dunbar
c. 1460–c. 1520
Poet

Background William Dunbar was born in East Lothian and probably attended St Andrews University between 1475 and 1479, but little else is known of his early life. He initially became a mendicant friar but found the life unsuitable.

Life at court In 1500 **James IV** granted him a pension to last either for life or until he received a church benefice which paid more, and for the next 13 years Dunbar lived at court, writing poems and petitioning for the benefice which James always refused to grant, preferring to keep his favoured poet with him. Dunbar also travelled on foreign embassies, including those to London to arrange the king's marriage with Margaret Tudor, daughter of Henry VII of England. His *The Thrissil and the Rois*, in praise of the royal couple, is one of his finest poems.

His poetry Dunbar's range of subjects was immense, and his poems are rich in their use of language and accomplishment. His subject matter and personality are reminiscent of **Burns**, with whom he shares a sympathetic and humourous attitude to life. His poems also show the same autobiographical concerns – seen in *On His Heid-ake*, a complaint about a migraine. But of all his writings, his satirical works are best; for example, his satire on epic poems of courtly love, *Tua Mariit Wemen and the Wedo*, in which women discuss men's sexual prowess. Dunbar's poetry was part of a flowering of culture in early-16th-century Scotland, and his dolorous *Lament for the Makaris*, reflecting on the deaths one by one of many of his fellow poets and on his fear of his own mortality, is one of his most evocative works.

After 1513 There is no record of Dunbar at court after the disaster of Flodden, and while his fate is unknown, it is most likely that the grieving queen granted his wish for a benefice.

Viscount Dundee
1648–1689
Royalist commander

John Graham of Claverhouse was known to posterity by two nicknames, Bloody Clavers and Bonnie Dundee. He got the first from his suppression of the Covenanters, and the second after **Scott** revived his reputation, and in honour of his exceptional beauty.

Battles with the Covenanters Like many sons of the Scots minor nobility, Claverhouse served as a professional soldier in the wars in Europe. He returned to Scotland in 1677 and joined a regiment being raised to stamp out the Covenanters in the south-west. The Covenanters at this time were the extremist rump of the presbyterian party and were seen as a threat to social order, especially after their murder of Archbishop Sharpe in 1679. It was a difficult struggle – Claverhouse was even obliged to take a search party out on his wedding day, much to his disgust – and one in which his success made him many dangerous enemies. Such was the venom with which he was hated that it was believed he was in league with the devil, and that bullets fired at him simply bounced off.

Flight from Edinburgh and Killiecrankie The precariousness of his position was evident in 1688 when James VII was deposed in England. One of the king's last acts was to reward the faithful Claverhouse with the title of Viscount Dundee. He took his place at the Edinburgh Convention of 1689 when the Scots met to decide the succession. An ill-advised letter from the king swung opinion against his cause, and Dundee, sensing personal danger, left the city with his men. He was proclaimed outlaw, but gained support in the Highlands where he waited for reinforcements to arrive from the king in Ireland. In July his forces decimated Government troops at the Pass of Killiecrankie, but Dundee was killed at the point of victory by a shot which struck him under his left arm; with him died James VII's cause in Scotland.

John Dunlop
1840–1921
Inventor and pioneer of the pneumatic tyre

Veterinary career John Boyd Dunlop was born into a farming
family at Dreghorn in Ayrshire. With such a background it is not
surprising that he was interested in veterinary surgery, and he
gained his diploma when he was 19 years old. He practised for
eight years in Edinburgh before moving in 1867 to Belfast where
his professional skills and personal qualities established his practice as one of the largest and most successful in Ireland.

Bicycle tyre for his son In 1887 Dunlop's nine-year-old son complained of the bumpiness of his tricycle ride on cobbled streets. To
solve the problem Dunlop inflated a rubber tube and fixed it to a
wooden wheel. As a test, he rolled it and one of the trike's solid
rubber wheels across a cobbled courtyard; the solid wheel did not
reach the opposite wall, but the pneumatic wheel rolled across easily and bounced back. He patented his invention in 1888.

Development of the tyre Dunlop asked a Belfast cycle manufacturer to modify the wheel to accommodate spokes, and had the
opportunity to see his invention tried out in 1889 at the cycle race
on Queen's College Sports Day. After suffering cries of 'pudding
tyres', Dunlop's rider, the captain of the local cycle club, had the
last laugh when he won easily. Among the beaten riders were the
sons of Harvey du Cros, a Dublin businessman who later bought
Dunlop's patent. Dunlop, already on the point of retiring from
practice, moved to Dublin to go into business with du Cros. (It
emerged that Robert Thomson, another Scot, had patented his
ultimately undeveloped invention of a pneumatic tyre in 1846,
although the company was able to patent its wheel fittings.) Sold
in 1896, the company later became the Dunlop Rubber Company
Ltd, but it did not make much money for Dunlop. He settled in
Dublin, ending his working life running a draper's business.

Duns Scotus
c. 1265–c.1308
Philosopher and theologian

Franciscan orders John Duns Scotus was among the greatest of medieval thinkers. He was probably born in the Berwickshire village of Duns, which he left to attend the Franciscan school at Dumfries. He was received into the Franciscan order in the town in 1281, taking the name of his birthplace as his own name, as was the custom, and was ordained into the priesthood in Northampton 10 years later.

Teaching career Duns Scotus studied at Oxford in the early 1290s, returning there from Paris several years later to teach. He was back teaching in Paris again around 1301, but was expelled from the city for taking the pope's part in a quarrel between the papacy and the French king. He returned briefly before moving to Cologne in 1307 where he taught for only a year before his death, reputedly from a stroke.

His ideas Duns Scotus' teachings were in part a reaction to the ideas of Thomas Aquinas, now regarded as the foremost philosopher and theologian of the medieval period. Unlike Aquinas, he believed in the primacy of the individual and of individual will, that will predominated over the intellect, and that faith itself was achieved through an act of will.

Theological rivalry The teachings of Duns Scotus split the Franciscans and Dominicans into two acrimonious rival camps who treated the other with contempt and hostility. Duns Scotus gained the name of 'doctor subtilis' because of the originality and penetrative nature of his intellect and ideas, and his understanding and criticism of Aquinas'. But he fell from favour in the 16th century, by when his followers had acquired the name 'Dunses', meant to denote their dullness and obstinacy, and from which evolved the modern word 'dunce'.

Grace Dalrymple Elliott
c. 1758–1823
Courtesan

Childhood and early marriage Grace was born in Edinburgh, the youngest daughter of Hew Dalrymple, a prominent advocate. Shortly after her birth her father left her mother, who returned to bring up her young family with her parents. Grace was sent to a convent in France to be educated, and on her return to Scotland in 1771 made her debut in Edinburgh society. She was so beautiful that her success was guaranteed, and she soon received and accepted a proposal of marriage from Dr John Elliott, a fashionable London Scottish physician 22 years her senior.

Temptation and fall Through her marriage Grace gained entry to the highest society circles. Hardly surprisingly, the adolescent bride lacked the judgement to withstand the temptations placed before her, and after a series of liaisons she finally ran off with Lord Valentia in 1774. (Elliott received a divorce and £12,000 damages.) She was tracked down by her brother and confined to a French convent but was quickly rescued and brought back to London by Lord Cholmondeley. Her course in life was set; she became the mistress of several prominent men, including Lords Valentia and Cholmondeley, Charles Windham, George Selwyn and the Prince of Wales (later George IV). When Grace had a daughter in 1782 several, including the prince, claimed paternity.

Life in revolutionary France The prince introduced Grace to the Duke of Orleans in 1784, and in 1786 she went to live in Paris. She stayed there during the 1790s, and after her death her granddaughter published her highly entertaining *Journal of My Life During the Revolution*. In it, she claimed to have been imprisoned in Paris four times, and to have acted as a go-between for Marie Antoinette and Louis XVIII. Napoleon was said to have proposed to her. She died at Ville d'Avray, mistress of the local mayor.

Alexander Fleming
1881–1955
Discoverer of penicillin

His legacy Alexander Fleming is famous for his discovery of penicillin, one of the single biggest drug advances in the history of medicine. The lives of innumerable people around the world in the past half-century have been saved by his discovery, which he ascribed to a 'triumph of accident and shrewd observation'.

Early career He was born at Lochfield in Ayrshire, the son of a farmer. His father died when Alexander was 13, and the boy went to London to live with his older brother. After leaving school he spent five years working as a shipping clerk before entering London University in 1901 as a medical student at St Mary's in Paddington, the hospital where he would spend the rest of his career. Fleming was an outstanding student, and after graduating in 1906 he joined the lab of the noted bacteriologist, Almroth Wright, who had admired both his medical skills and his talents as a marksman in the university rifle team.

War experience and its lessons Fleming's career was interrupted by service in the Royal Medical Army Corps during the First World War. He saw at first hand the deaths from infected wounds of many soldiers, and the experience heightened an interest he already had in the treatment of bacterial infection. In 1922 he discovered the antibacterial properties of lysozyme, a substance naturally present in secretions of the human body – for example, in tears. Its efficacy was limited, but the crucial principle of a substance which could destroy bacteria yet be harmless to human cells was further reinforced for Fleming.

Discovery of *Penicillum notatum* In 1928 Fleming noticed that a culture of staphylococcus bacteria which he had been growing had accidentally become infected with mould. But what made it remarkable was that the staphylococci around the mould had been totally destroyed. Fleming identified the mould as *Penicillum notatum*, which commonly grows on stale food, and research confirmed its unprecedented antibacterial properties and harmlessness to human cells.

Commercial development But limited technical awareness and difficulties in stabilising and producing this fragile substance meant that penicillin, as Fleming named the drug, could not be produced commercially. It took another 15 years until a team of Oxford scientists led by Howard Florey and Ernst Chain developed a method of manufacture to make the drug widely available. From 1943 to 1945 all supplies of the new drug were detailed for use solely by the armed services, so that many of those fighting in the Second World War were able to overcome the problem of infected wounds which had so impressed itself on Fleming during the First World War.

Honours Fleming, Florey and Chain were jointly awarded the Nobel Prize for Physiology or Medicine in 1945, and Fleming was showered with numerous other honours from around the world. Yet he always remained a modest man, and never attempted to patent his discovery, in the hope that it could be as cheap, plentiful and efficacious as possible.

Bill Forsyth
Born 1946
Film-maker

Early career The standard-bearer of a new Scottish film industry, Bill Forsyth was born in Glasgow in 1946. He became involved in the film industry immediately after leaving school in 1963, when he worked as an apprentice to a documentary film-maker. He continued making films on his own after his employer died, and in 1970 he entered the National Film School in London. However, he was an early drop-out, and had returned to Glasgow by the following year.

First movies and fame at home Forsyth first came to widespread public attention in 1979, when his film *That Sinking Feeling*, about the money-making attempts of a group of unemployed teenagers in Glasgow, was warmly received at the Edinburgh Film Festival. His follow-up, *Gregory's Girl*, a teenage comedy romance, gained him fame in Britain, although it was thought necessary to sub-title the film for its trip across the Atlantic.

US recognition In 1983 *Local Hero*, which starred Burt Lancaster, was his first US feature, and it fully established Forsyth as a film-maker in both in Britain and the US. This was a classic film F mould of *Whisky Galore*, a timeless and seminal story of w natives outsmarting a big-city incomer. (Incidentally, *Local* was one of the inspirations for the gently weird *Northern Expe* TV series.) After *Comfort and Joy* the following year Forsyth time in North America, producing *Housekeeping* and *Breaking* . However, he did not personally enjoy his time abroad, and returned to Britain. In 1994 he released his latest feature, *Being Human*, with American star Robin Williams.

James Frazer
1854–1941
Anthropologist

James George Frazer was a Glaswegian, born on 1 January 1854. He first attended Glasgow University, then Cambridge, where he became a classics fellow.

His ideas on human customs Frazer's studies in classical scholarship developed into an interest in social anthropology. He believed that human attempts to understand, come to terms with and control the social and material environment gave rise to the development of successive systems and patterns of beliefs and customs. According to this theory, magic was initially used in an attempt to gain some control over the natural world. This was followed by a belief in appeasable gods, then by religion and then by science. Throughout this succession, ideas were constantly being reinterpreted according to prevailing theories.

Influence of his work Frazer published his theories in *The Golden Bough: A Study in Comparative Religion*. It first appeared in 1890 and went through a succession of constantly revised versions, reaching its climax in the 12 volumes published in 1915, although Frazer was still adding material in 1936. His books were stuffed with examples of customs and practices from around the world, and these provided great inspiration for many writers, including Conrad, Eliot, Lawrence and Yeats. Their exotic nature meant that the books were also a great popular success. However, the ideas behind Frazer's work were completely in line with theories of evolution from the 19th century, with the result that it seemed slightly dated when it was published. Consequently, despite his popular success, he received no great acclaim from his peers. Frazer was professor of social anthropology at Liverpool, then Cambridge from 1908. His wife died hours after him in 1941.

Lewis Grassic Gibbon
1901–1935
Writer

Youth   James Leslie Mitchell, who later chose the pen-name of
Lewis Grassic Gibbon, was born on an Aberdeenshire farm at the
turn of the century. He left school early to take up a job as a newspaper reporter and as a teenager was so inspired by the Bolshevik
Revolution in Russia that he joined the Communist Party.

Army service   The main years of Mitchell's working life were spent
in the armed services: from 1919 to 1923 he was with the Royal
Army Service Corps in Persia, India and Egypt. He tried for several months after his release to write for a living, but lack of
money ultimately forced his re-enlistment, this time as a clerk in
the RAF for a further six years.

Successful literary career   From just before his release in 1929,
Mitchell achieved some success in getting his work into print, and
from then until 1935 his output was prolific, with 18 books published on a wide range of subjects, from prehistoric and archaeo-
logical material to science fiction and historical novels; he also
published a biography of the explorer Mungo **Park**. Most of these
appeared in his own name, but it is for the trilogy *A Scots Quair*,
published under his pseudonym, that he is best remembered.
These deeply symbolic works – *Sunset Song*, *Cloud Howe* and *Grey
Granite* – look at the land and the upheaval affecting the country
way of life through the character of Chris Guthrie, a crofter's
daughter from north-east Scotland. The books' dialogue attempts
to convey the patterns of local speech, making them both innovative and evocative. Mitchell settled in Welwyn Garden City after
1929, far enough away from the north-east to allow him the necessary dispassion for his writings. It was there he died, tragically
early, from a perforated ulcer.

The Glasgow Boys
1880–c. 1910
Artists

The Glasgow Boys were a group of painters who burst upon the
fine art scene in the 1880s, establishing a revolutionary, modern
painting style for the late 19th century.

Philosophy As a radical artistic movement, they consciously
rebelled against the contemporary establishment in both aesthetic
and political terms. They were influenced greatly by contemporary French painting (many of them travelled to France to study)
which was more simple and realistic in its approach, with a more
direct and bold painting method and depiction of subject. This
simplicity was extended to their artistic philosophy, too, in the
belief that a painting should be complete in itself and not an alle-
gory or symbol of some story. Their painting was intended to
upset the stuffy Scottish artistic establishment, and it did. The
Boys opposed institutions such as the
Royal Scottish Academy and, for lack
of exhibition space and patronage,
they were forced to show their paintings in London and Europe, where
they were enthusiastically received.

Examples of best work This imme-
diacy of approach to both medium
and subject led them to a preference
for genre painting, with ordinary subjects taken from everyday Scottish
life. This is seen in its finest form
in James Guthrie's *A Hind's
Daughter* (1883) and W. Y.
Macgregor's *The Vegetable
Stall* (1884).

Who they were The Boys themselves were not a group of equals, but rather several little bands whose main leaders – James Guthrie (opposite), W. Y. Macgregor (right) and John Lavery – tended to draw others into their circles. It was not always clear who was a member of the group – even the painters themselves quarrelled over that – but other members did include artists such as J. Whitelaw Hamilton, E. A. Walton, Joseph Crawhall, E. A. Hornel and George Henry.

Nor were they particularly associated with Glasgow: they did not paint much in the way of city scenes, often preferring the backgrounds of their own parts of the country. But the group, with its collection of exceptionally talented individuals, was brilliant, and the work which they produced, especially in the 1880s and '90s, was exceptional.

Later work and professional success Almost inevitably, their success ensured their assumption into the establishment which they had fought so hard against: their original style became the accepted Scottish artistic style of the early 20th century, while their own later work was modified by other influences then in vogue, including the Arts and Crafts movement, leading them to a more subtle and less direct form of painting. In addition, the former rebels themselves became guardians of the establishment – Guthrie was appointed president of the RSA in 1902, and he and Lavery were later knighted.

The Glasgow Girls
c. 1890–1920
Artists

The Glasgow Girls were a group of artists and designers primarily known as the main exponents of the decorative arts and design movement called the Glasgow Style. Although their work was crucial to Scottish art and design in the past century, their contributions went unacknowledged until recently, when they were brought to public attention again.

Background The Glasgow Girls were a loosely connected group of individuals who met and were influenced by each other's work at the Glasgow School of Art under the enlightened headship of Francis Newbery. His talented leadership and progressive curriculum gained the Glasgow school international renown. At a time when university education was largely closed to women, he encouraged students of both sexes to work together in almost all classes and created an atmosphere in which unconventional talent, such as that of the **Glasgow Boys** or Charles Rennie **Mackintosh**, could flourish. Under these circumstances, greater numbers of women enrolled in the school and helped to create a movement and style which was both innovative totally unique.

Influences Among the important influences on the Glasgow Style were the Arts and Crafts movement and Art Nouveau; on a more local level, echoes can also be seen of Celtic art. The most important motifs used were plants and flowers (as in the Glasgow Rose, for example) and fine, elongated female forms. Although the influences and subject matter reflected the strong links with Art Nouveau, the resulting work was more severe and rectilinear, and closer to the Viennese and German Secessionists whom they influenced greatly. The Glaswegian artists and designers also eschewed the worthiness of the Arts and Crafts movement for a more purely aesthetic approach.

Who they were The Girls worked in most of the accepted media of the day: fabrics and embroidery, wood, metal and ceramics, oil and watercolour. Jessie Rowat Newbery, Francis' wife, and Anne Macbeth revived the much-undervalued art of embroidery and needlework at the art school. More unusually, De Courcy Dewar became one of the few women working with metals and enamels at the time. Margaret Macdonald (opposite) and her sister, Frances, were studying at the school when they were introduced by Francis Newbery to two evening students with styles similar to theirs: Charles Rennie Mackintosh, who became the leading light of the Glasgow Style, and his friend and fellow-architect, Herbert MacNair. The sisters later married the two friends and The Four, as they became known, worked and exhibited together. Another prominent member was Jessie M. King (above), initially an illustrator and book designer with a highly distinctive fantasy style. She later moved into a much wider range of media, including metalworking, stained glass, interior and furniture design and fabric printing. While the movement was design-based, painters such as Bessie MacNicol and Norah Neilson Gray, who came to the school slightly later, were also included among their numbers.

David Gregory
1627–1720
Physician and inventor

Hereditary genius David Gregory was born at Drumoak near Aberdeen where his father, a minister, had been deposed and imprisoned by the Covenanters. His mother's family, the Andersons, were mathematical geniuses, and she brought that talent to the Gregorys who for four generations and beyond produced a series of mathematicians and physicians. David Gregory was apprenticed early on to a Dutch merchant but came home in 1655 and took possession of the estate of Kinardie north of Aberdeen after the death of his brother.

Farming, medicine and meteorology Gregory led a life which would be considered remarkable by many standards. Although a landowner, he knew nothing of farming, for which he was ridiculed by his neighbours. However, his other talents meant that he was also regarded with some awe. Foremost among these were his medical skills. He spent much of the day engaged in consulting and usually went to bed in the early evening, getting up again at 3 am to study and work. The reason for such odd hours may have been the need for some peace and quiet – Gregory was the father of 32 children by two wives. Although he attracted rich and poor patients from miles away, he refused to take a fee from anyone. He was also the first person in the area to have a barometer, and attracted suspicion of dabbling in witchcraft because of the accuracy of his weather forecasts.

Artillery invention In the early 18th century Gregory became interested in artillery, and constructed a cannon of his own invention. He sent it to his son, also David, by then astronomy professor at Oxford, who showed the cannon to Isaac Newton. Newton was so horrified at its destructive potential that he urged David to dismantle it. No trace of it was ever found.

John Grierson
1898–1972
Film-maker

His standing John Grierson was a pioneering figure in non-fiction film-making and one of the greatest directors and producers of his day. The first to use the term 'documentary', in a film review, he later became known as 'the father of documentary'.

Education Grierson was born in Stirlingshire and educated at Glasgow University. After graduating he went to the US to spend three more years studying communications.

Early work He returned in 1927 and asked the Empire Marketing Board to research film's potential propaganda value. The board responded by asking him to form a film unit for them. His first work, *Drifters*, about herring fishermen, was a success and allowed him to recruit a talented team. In 1933 when the EMB was wound up the team was transferred to the GPO where he did some of his most famous work, including the superb *Night Mail*, with commentary by W. H. Auden. Grierson also brought some world-famous and innovative directors, including Robert Flaherty and Alberto Cavalcanti, to work for the unit. The films he produced at this time seemed to herald a new, documentary film movement.

International career During the Second World War Grierson headed the National Film Board of Canada and established other supervisory panels in Australia, New Zealand and Scotland. He was appointed head of film and communications with UNESCO in 1946, then with the Central Office of Information in 1948. He also worked with the National Film Finance Corporation.

Personality Primarily a producer from the mid 1930s onwards, Grierson remained a towering figure in film documentary. For him, documentary liberated film from the constraints of both studio and actors. He was a supremely self-confident man who established the genre but who alienated as many people as he attracted.

Douglas Haig
1861–1928
First World War commander

Douglas Haig was born in Edinburgh into an old Borders family. He was educated at Oxford University, then at the Royal Military College at Sandhurst.

Career in Africa   He joined the 7th Hussars in 1885 and saw active service in British colonial wars at the end of the 19th century. He was in Egypt in the Omdurman campaign in 1898, when he commanded a wing of the last cavalry charge in battle, and in South Africa in the Boer War (1899–1902), by the end of which he was chief staff officer in the cavalry division. Haig subsequently joined the general staff, on which he held several posts, including, from 1911, that of GOC Aldershot. This position carried with it command of the 1st Army Corps should the British Expeditionary Force be mobilised.

The Western Front   Consequently, Haig had this command when war broke out in 1914, and took over as commander-in-chief the following year. As such, he was responsible for the policy of attrition which was followed to the exclusion of any other strategy by the British forces on the Western Front for the next three years. It cost the lives of almost a million British troops alone, and its use has been the subject of great controversy ever since. Haig's troops halted what turned out to be the final German offensive in the summer of 1918, and he advised the Allied counter-offensive which ended the war in November. He received many honours and was made first Earl Haig of Bemersyde.

Later life   After the war Haig organised the Royal British Legion, which helped former soldiers. As a member of the famous whisky family, he had continued to look after the company's interests throughout his military career, and he was a director of the Distillers Company Ltd until his death.

Duke of Hamilton
1606–1649
Royalist soldier

Early royal favour James Hamilton succeeded to his father's title of marquess at the age of 19. He had been married at 13 to a girl of 7, and was sent to Oxford to study thereafter. He found himself much in favour with Charles I after the king's accession in 1626, and this was marked in 1643 when Charles created him duke, making him the foremost noble in the land.

Between king and Covenanters Hamilton's first military encounter was a failure: he led a force of 6000 men off to fight for Gustavus Adolphus of Sweden in the Thirty Years' War, but was back home in two years. Despite his failure he became one of Charles' foremost advisers in Scottish affairs, and tried to guide the king out of the religious minefield which his policies had created. He walked a tightrope between, on the one hand, the king and, on the other, the signatories of the National Covenant, who rejected the new prayer book and the changes the king was attempting to introduce to the Scottish Church. However, his attempts to mediate lost him friends on both sides: the Marquess of **Montrose** distrusted Hamilton and criticised him to the king, who preferred Montrose's confrontational approach to the compromise advocated by Hamilton. He fell from favour and was imprisoned from 1644 to 1646.

Invasion of England Liberated by the Parliamentarians, he returned to his policy of conciliation. In 1647 the king, who had fallen into the hands first of the Parliamentarians and then of the army, agreed finally to accept presbyterianism in Scotland, in return for which a Scots army would come to England to rescue him. In 1648 Hamilton led south a force of 20,000 which was defeated at Preston by Cromwell's army of 9000 men. He was tried in London and executed the following year, like his master.

Patrick Hamilton
1503–1528
Lutheran martyr

Patrick Hamilton was Scotland's first Protestant martyr. He was born probably at Stonehouse in Lanarkshire, and was a great-grandson of James II.

Attraction to Lutheranism In 1518 Patrick went to study at Paris. Martin Luther's writings were burnt at the university there in 1521, so this was probably where Hamilton first encountered his teachings. After a stay at Louvain he was back in Scotland in 1523. While still within the Church, he began publicly to show his sympathy for the reformed ideas, thus attracting the attention of the church authorities. Hamilton thought it wise to leave the country early in 1527 and he travelled to Wittenburg where he met Luther and Melancthon. He studied briefly at the new Protestant university of Marburg, and wrote an exposition of Luther's teachings, *Loci Communes*, which became known as *Patrick's Places*. By autumn of that year he was back in Scotland where, following the example of Luther's personal statement against celibacy, he married.

Trial and martyrdom In January 1528 Hamilton was invited by Cardinal Beaton to a conference at St Andrews, about which he felt a sense of foreboding even before he set out. After meeting with the cardinal, Hamilton was allowed to preach in the town for a month before he was seized, tried and convicted of heresy. On 29 February sentence of death was pronounced and carried out. Hamilton was burned at the stake in front of St Salvator's College. His death was slow and agonising; not enough fuel had been brought, and it took six hours and a refuelling of the fire for his whole body to be consumed. His martyrdom did as much to publicise Lutheran ideas as his life would have done, and his work became widely available after his death.

Keir Hardie
1836–1915
Socialist and labour leader

Early life and influences James Keir Hardie, born near Holytown, was the eldest of nine children and had to help support his family from very early childhood; by the age of 10 he was already working in the Lanarkshire pits. As a result, he never attended school formally and was taught to read by his mother, who also instilled in him the Christian values which were always so influential to his thought and work.

Labour and temperance activities By the time he was 22, Hardie had been blacklisted by local mine-owners because of his activities in organising the workers to help get better wages, improved safety and better housing. He was also active in the temperance movement, where he met his wife. The couple married and moved to Cumnock in Ayrshire, where Hardie continued his attempts to organise miners throughout the country while supporting his family by working as a journalist.

Labour in politics Hardie was a Liberal until now, but by 1887 he was convinced of the need for a distinct organisation to represent the interests of working people, and the following year he founded the Scottish Labour Party, the first independent party for labour in Britain. The same year he stood as its first candidate and was defeated in the election at Mid-Lanark. Meanwhile, he was editing his own newspapers: in 1887 he had founded *The Miner*, which in 1888 became *The Labour Leader*. These helped increase his influence in labour politics throughout the 1880s. Electoral success finally came in 1892, when he was returned as MP for West Ham South in London. Much to the scandal of his fellow MPs, Hardie arrived at the House of Commons wearing a tweeds and a cloth cap rather than the formal day suit and silk hat then considered necessary for the conduct of Parliamentary business.

Hardie was by now one of the most hated men in the country; his labour-organising activities, his dress, his appearance and his plain Scots language were all causes of fear and hatred in many. Yet he was a practical rather than theoretical politician, and was always portrayed as more extreme than he really was.

Formation of the Labour Party In 1893 the Independent Labour Party was formed, merging with the Scottish Labour Party, and Hardie became its first chairman. He lost his seat at West Ham in 1895, but in the election of 1900 was returned at Merthyr Tydfil, which he represented to the end of his life. 1900 was an auspicious year for Hardie: he saw the realisation of his hopes for parliamentary representation when the Trades Union Congress formed the Labour Representation Committee to get more Labour MPs into parliament. Within six years there were 29, and the modern Labour Party had begun.

His legacy Hardie died in 1915, his heart and health broken by the outbreak of a war which an international network of socialist movements had been powerless to stop. He spent his life working for better conditions for ordinary people, championing, among other causes, votes for women and Home Rule for Ireland. His legacy to history, however, was his influence over labour politics and the party which was its expression. More than anyone, he created the political labour movement and shaped its distinctive character of an alliance of socialists and trade unionists.

Thomas Henderson
1789–1844
Astronomer

Education Born in Dundee, Thomas was the youngest of five children of a tradesman father. He did well at school, where he showed a particular aptitude for mathematics. At the age of 15 he took a post as clerk in his native city but at 21 he moved to Edinburgh to take up a legal apprenticeship.

Love of astronomy Despite his pursuit of a legal career, however, Henderson's real love was astronomy, and he spent much of his leisure time engaged on astronomical calculation. He soon made a name for himself in astronomical circles, and in 1831 he was invited to take up the post of astronomer in the observatory at the Cape of Good Hope. In spite of his chronically poor health and his bad eyesight, he spent a year in the inhospitable terrain of the Cape, struggling with a poorly equipped observatory before returning home in 1832 with a mass of information to be analysed and published. That year also saw his greatest achievement, in measuring the parallax of the star closest to Earth, Alpha Centauri. In 1844 he was appointed professor of astronomy at Edinburgh University, first Astronomer Royal for Scotland, and took charge of the old observatory on Calton Hill in Edinburgh.

Money and health problems Having been an archetypal enthusiastic amateur for most of his career, Henderson made little money from astronomy. His health did not improve (he suffered from heart disease, and in the last weeks of his life was unable to climb up Calton Hill to his observatory) and he never recovered from the death of his wife in 1842. He died two years later, leaving their two-year-old daughter orphaned. She received little in the way of inheritance from her father, although she later inherited a fortune from her maternal uncle.

David Octavius Hill
1802–1870
Painter and photographer

David Octavius Hill was born in Perth in 1802, and showed artistic promise from a very early age. He was educated at Perth Academy and Edinburgh's School of Design.

Early painting career   His particular interests were in landscape and later portrait painting, and in 1821 his *Sketches of Scenery in Perthshire*, among the first sets of lithographs to appear in Scotland, was published. He was one of the leading lights of the Scottish Academy which he helped found in 1829 and whose secretary he became the following year.

Move into photography   In 1843 Hill, now an established portrait painter, undertook the painting of the members of the Church of Scotland who had broken away, led by Thomas **Chalmers**, in the Disruption of that year, to form the Free Church of Scotland. He was concerned about how to record the features of those involved in the Disruption, and in the course of his researches met and went into partnership with Robert Adamson (1821–48), a recently established and successful photographer. The pair made calotype portraits of all the clergy and laity involved in the new Church, which were later used by Hill for his monumental *The Signing of the Deed of Demission*. Hill and Adamson recognised the importance of their photography in its own right, and not simply as a means to aid portrait painting.

Partnership with Adamson   Hill's association with Anderson, cut short by his partner's untimely death, produced around 2000 calotypes. They took portrait photographs and shots of landscapes and buildings around Edinburgh. Their study, *The Fishermen and Women of the Firth of Forth*, recording life in Newhaven, was the first major use of photography as a social and documentary tool.

James Hogg
1770–1835
Writer

Child shepherd James Hogg, the 'Ettrick Shepherd', was the second of four sons of a Borders farming family. They were not well off, and the young James was sent out to herd sheep when he was only six years old. He received almost no formal schooling; instead, his education came from the Bible and catechism and the ballads he was taught by his mother.

Literary ups and downs His first publication came in 1801, when he had *Scottish Pastorals* printed up in Edinburgh while he was in the city selling sheep. It was not a success. The following year he was introduced to Walter **Scott**, with whom he remained friends for the rest of his life. Over the next decade he published several works, including one on sheep diseases, making enough money to buy a farm then promptly going bankrupt. In 1813 he had his first real poetical success with *The Queen's Wake*, and in 1816 he received the bequest of a farm from the Duchess of Buccleuch, an old patron. This allowed him to concentrate fully on writing, and he produced some of his best material from then on. Throughout the 1820s Hogg was a main contributor to *Blackwood's Magazine*. He was content to live on his farm with his family, and although he kept in touch with Edinburgh literary society – such as when Scott and other friends came to visit – he preferred the country life, and refused to go to Edinburgh for the visit of George IV in 1822 because it took place on the same day as the annual Borders fair.

A Justified Sinner Hogg's most famous book today is *The Private Memoirs and Confessions of a Justified Sinner*. Written in 1824, it deals with the very Scottish literary theme of duality and is an extraordinary and disturbing book of great power. It was not well received by contemporaries, who regarded it with distaste.

David Hume
1711–1776
Philosopher

Youthful philosopher   One of the world's great philosophers, David Hume was a product of the era of the Enlightenment in Scotland. He was born in Edinburgh, the second of three children of a Borders family of minor nobility. His father died early in David's childhood, and the children were brought up by their devoted mother. He went to Edinburgh University when he was 12, intending to read law, but philosophy was his main interest even then, and he changed subjects half-way through his course.

Publications   He suffered depression as an adolescent, and took off, first to Bristol and then to France, where he spent three years in Anjou from 1734. It was during this time that he wrote his philosophical masterpiece, *Treatise of Human Nature*, expounding his empiricist worldview. Despite the brilliance of the work's contribution to contemporary philosophical debate, 'it fell deadborn from the press' in 1739, as its mortified author noted. Hume was back on his family's Berwickshire estate for the publication of *Essays, Moral and Political*, in 1741. This second work was much better received, and gained him critical recognition.

Career hampered by agnosticism   However, his sceptical views on religion, which amounted to agnosticism, effectively debarred him from two important academic appointments in the following decade – the moral philosophy chair at Edinburgh, and the chair of logic vacated by his close friend, Adam **Smith**, at Glasgow. Instead, he spent the period working as a tutor and travelling abroad on diplomatic missions.

Histories and other work   After his failure to acquire the Glasgow professorship, Hume became keeper of the Advocates' Library in Edinburgh from 1752 to 1757. This gave him the research facilities he needed to complete his *History of England*, a five-volume work dating back from 1688 to Roman times. It was published in 1761. His international reputation was high by now: not only was he an original philosopher, he also dealt in theoretical and practical politics, history and economics. He received various civil service appointments throughout the 1760s, including one in Paris, which he loved. He retired to Edinburgh in 1768, and died eight years later of bowel cancer.

Pleasant personality By common account of all his contemporaries, Hume was a most affable man, cheerful and good-natured to those he encountered. When in Paris he expressed his pleasure at being feted on account of his personality more than on his literary works. He enjoyed simple pleasures such as cooking, and was inordinately fond of eating and drinking, especially with friends. As a consequence he grew to be very stout in later life, and once fell into a bog from which, on account of his great weight, he could not escape. A passing woman agreed to rescue him only on condition that he should first recite the Lord's Prayer. Much to the annoyance of many religious people of the time, Hume died a peaceful death. Adam Smith said of his friend that he had been as close to the 'character of a perfectly wise and virtuous man as perhaps the nature of human frailty would permit'.

John and William Hunter
John 1728–1793; William 1718–1783
Anatomists

Both born at Long Calderwood in East Kilbride, the Hunter brothers, William and more especially John made notable contributions to the study of anatomy and surgery in the 18th century.

William's spectacular success William (left) received the benefits of the education which his parents could afford, first studying divinity at Glasgow University, and subsequently abandoning it for medicine in 1737. Four years later he moved to London, where he trained in anatomy at St George's Hospital. By 1748 he was specialising in obstetrics, and had found great fame for the quality of his lectures. In the same year he used his influence in the hospital to get a place for his brother, John (opposite), as his dissection assistant.

John's early lack of promise John, the youngest of the family, had never shown any aptitude for books, preferring instead to roam the countryside. His lack of a proper education was to be a difficulty throughout his life, and one which he never overcame completely. He always found reading difficult, and the vast knowledge which he ultimately acquired was the fruit almost entirely of his own researches and experience.

Brothers' careers and quarrels John spent 12 years working as his brother's assistant, helping him with his lectures and dissections and learning surgery at the same time. However, as well as having the more talented and original mind, John had an overbearing and abrasive personality, and the two brothers quarrelled in 1760. John left to join the army, but on his return he quickly established his name as the foremost surgeon of his day and was appointed surgeon extraordinary to George III in 1776. William, too, had reached the heights of his profession; by now he had made his name in obstetrics and had been appointed physician extraordinary to Queen Charlotte and professor of anatomy to the Royal Academy. However, in 1780 the two brothers were further estranged when they quarrelled publicly over who had made a particular discovery, and they were barely on speaking terms by the time of William's death three years later.

John's collections The advances John made from his obsessive interest in dissection were ground-breaking, and they genuinely advanced contemporary knowledge on several subjects, such as dentistry, sexually transmitted diseases, embryology, haematology, inflammation and gunshot wounds. He also made surgery a science, raising its status from that of a barber's profession. John also built up an enormous museum of over 10,000 exhibits of comparative anatomy. The Government bought it and presented it to the Royal College of Surgeons, but it was largely destroyed in an air-raid during the Second World War. William's more eclectic collection of anatomical specimens, minerals, coins and medals, together with his library, was bequeathed to Glasgow University.

James Hutton
1726–1797
Founder of modern geological science

Varied early career   A native of Edinburgh, James Hutton was educated at the university there before joining a legal firm as apprentice at the age of 17. An interest in chemistry was already apparent, however, and he was fired after his employer discovered his room being used as a laboratory. More study, this time in medicine, at Edinburgh, Paris and Leiden, followed, before James decided in 1750 that a medical career was not for him and opted instead for farming. He lived in Norfolk to learn farming and spent time travelling in the Low Countries before returning in 1754 to work a small family estate in Berwickshire.

Interest in geology   His experience as a farmer raised questions in his mind about the nature of the Earth and its rocks, and this gradually became a preoccupation. His discovery, with a friend, of a method of sal ammoniac manufacture from soot, gave him enough money to move to Edinburgh in 1768 and devote himself to research. Hutton deduced that the earth was igneous in origin and nature, and that no other forces were responsible for shaping it than those which were still continuing. His views were in line with those of Galileo, Newton and other great scientists: that the Earth and Universe were governed by a series of laws. His ideas led many – although not Hutton himself – to question the existence of God. He presented his findings to the Royal Society of Edinburgh in 1785, and published them in his most important work, *The Theory of the Earth*. Geology as a science had not existed before Hutton but his work changed that, establishing Edinburgh as a centre of geological research.

Personality and friendships   A kindly, sociable man, Hutton was one of a glittering circle of Edinburgh intellectuals, numbering among his friends Joseph **Black** and Adam **Smith**.

Elsie Inglis
1864–1917
Medical reformer and suffragette

Elsie Maud Inglis was the daughter of an employee of the East India Company and was born in India. Her family only returned to Edinburgh after her father's retirement in 1878. Her father was a constant support for her in her choice of career.

Difficulties for women in medicine   Elsie studied medicine at Edinburgh and Dublin, qualifying at Glasgow in 1892 where she studied under **MacEwen** who fired her interest in surgery. Women had only recently been allowed to study medicine, and there was great residual bitterness against them. Elsie returned in 1892 to Edinburgh and established only the second women's medical school (the first was closed). She became surgeon at Bruntsfield Hospital but her experience of prejudice from male colleagues, together with a pitiful lack of decent maternity facilities, led her in 1901 to establish a maternity hospital staffed entirely by women (later the Elsie Inglis Memorial Maternity Hospital).

Experiences in Serbia   Elsie joined the women's suffrage movement, and in 1906 founded the Scottish Women's Suffrage Federation. It was at a federation committee meeting in 1914 that the idea arose of sending mobile surgical units staffed by women, out to the war in Europe. Elsie was the driving force behind the organisation of the units, the first of which left for France in 1914 and Serbia in 1915. She went out to Serbia the same year, working in almost impossible conditions, the units constantly being pushed back by advancing Austrian forces. Her capture and subsequent repatriation early in 1916 did not daunt her, and in 1917 she was back at the front, this time in Russia, helping to care for wounded Serbs there. But the heavy workload, combined with the cold and lack of proper clothing and food finally combined to break her health and energy, and she died in November.

James I
1394–1437
King of Scots

Captivity in England James was born in Dunfermline, the second son of Robert III. After the murder of James' elder brother by his uncle, the Duke of Albany, in 1406, the king sent his younger son to France for safety. But en route the prince's ship fell into the hands of English pirates who took him to the court of the English king, where he was to be held, half prisoner, half paying guest, for the next 18 years. The ailing Robert III died, apparently of shock, on hearing the news of his son's fate.

Vigorous government James' eventual return to his kingdom in 1424 heralded the return of effective government in Scotland for the first time in over 30 years. He was the first in a series of effective and intelligent Stewart kings who energetically took royal authority to all corners of the country. Government and administration, the Church, finance, trade, agriculture, internal security and even sport (with the encouraging of archery and the banning of football and golf) were all dealt with in the mass of reforming legislation of James' early parliaments.

Royal avarice and noble unease However, James' great energy meant that he often lacked the judgement of knowing when to stop. This trait was compounded by his avariciousness in appropriating wealth for the Crown; he was seen to be guilty of spending profligately the money raised to pay his English ransom, an error of judgement which caused much resentment. Many nobles were also uneasy at his summary execution of his relatives, members of the Albany Stewart family, who had been implicated in the murder of his brother and in the disorder in the country after the death of Robert III. After the executions, James appropriated their lands for the Crown. The lands of other nobles followed, raising fears of what the king's next actions would be. James became deeply unpopular among the nobility.

Regicide In 1436 James and his court travelled to Perth to spend the Christmas season at the Blackfriars Abbey in the city. In the late night or early morning of 21 February 1437, while he was talking by the fire with his wife and her ladies-in-waiting, assassins broke into the abbey. One of the queen's ladies, Catherine Douglas, hearing men running up the stairs, barred the door with her arm to allow the king time to escape by climbing into a cellar. He was trapped there, however, and, despite overcoming two of his assailants, died after receiving 28 stab wounds to his body. His successor was his six-year-old son, now **James II**.

James' love for his wife As well as being a vigorous king, James I was a talented poet. His most famous work, *The Kingis Quair*, is a poem of love for his wife, Joan Beaufort, the daughter of the Earl of Somerset, whom he met and married while in England. James and Joan had six daughters and two sons. Theirs was a very happy marriage, and James's love for his wife was enduring: almost unique for a king, he had no mistresses or bastards. After his murder, his queen took a savage revenge on his assassins, who were tortured and executed with great brutality.

James II
1430–1460
King of Scots

Early succession James was born at Holyrood and was one of twin sons of **James I** and his wife, Joan. James' brother, Alexander, died early in life, leaving James as the sole male successor to the Scottish throne. He became king in 1437 at the age of six years. His mother acted as regent for a time, but by 1439 she felt sufficiently threatened to place herself and her son under the protection of one of the nobility, Sir Alexander Livingston.

Ruthless assertion of royal authority The families of Livingston and Douglas exploited for their own ends the disorder attendant on the minority, and after James assumed personal authority in 1450, he crushed both. The Livingstons were almost all executed or imprisoned by the end of the year, and by 1455 the king had systematically destroyed the unprecedented power held by the Douglases in the Borders and in the north, laying waste their lands and flattening their castles. The quarrel reached a dramatic and bloody climax in February 1452 when James lured the eighth Earl of Douglas to a dinner at Stirling Castle where he challenged him with treason and personally stabbed him to death. The earl's seat at Threave was reduced by James' new super-cannon, Mons Meg, imported specially from Flanders (the cannon can still be seen today at Edinburgh Castle).

Wise rule James' efficient suppression of his over-powerful nobles restored the political balance of power in the kingdom. It was consolidated by his good government, with legal reforms and the re-enactment of several of his father's laws. Like most Stewart kings, he was popular with the ordinary people, and Scotland enjoyed a short-lived period of peace and prosperity before he was killed in a freak accident, by an exploding cannon. He was succeeded by his nine-year-old son, now **James III**.

James III
1451–1488
King of Scots

Minority James was born at St Andrews and became king at nine years old after the death of his father, **James II**, in 1460. The nine-year period of his minority was not as troubled as his father's and grandfather's had been, but as usual one family – this time the Boyds – profited from the political imbalance. In 1469 the young king married Margaret, daughter of Christian I of Denmark. Her dowry included Orkney and Shetland, and the islands remained thereafter in Scottish control. In the same year James began to assert his personal authority, and the Boyds fell from power.

Mixed fortunes James, while a vigorous ruler, was not as successful at managing the nobility as some of the other Stewarts. He was seen as avaricious, with demands for taxes and a debasement of the coinage. He alienated many by not granting land and offices wisely, and was warned by his Parliament that he was not paying enough attention to matters at home. His foreign policy, which involved making peace with England, the ancient enemy, was certainly far-sighted but was also unpopular. More recklessly, he planned to invade the Low Countries. He was, however, like most Stewart kings, a lover of the arts, an attribute inherited by his eldest son, the future **James IV**, with spectacular results.

Noble revolt When peace with England began to unravel in 1480 and war threatened, some nobles fired a warning shot across the king's bows by seizing and hanging some of his favourites. It was a warning which he unwisely did not heed, and another rebellion followed in 1488. There were not many active rebels, but they did include the king's son, James. Father and son took the field against one another at Sauchieburn, both flying the royal standard. The rebellion went drastically wrong when the king was murdered after fleeing the battlefield, leaving his remorseful son as king.

James IV
1473–1513
King of Scots

Promise cut short James IV – charismatic, intelligent, well educated and good-looking – is the most glamorous king ever to have occupied the Scots throne. His reign was one of the most effective, prosperous and successful Scotland ever witnessed, he took the country almost into the first rank of European powers, and he kept one of the foremost courts of his day. Yet all this was cut short prematurely when he and many of his nobles died in pointless and muddy defeat at Flodden in September 1513.

Inglorious succession James was born, probably at Stirling, on 17 March 1473. He succeeded to the throne at 15 years of age after a rebellion against his father, **James III**, and although still young he assumed personal power immediately. His participation, albeit unwittingly, in his father's death, was something for which he never forgave himself, and he wore an iron belt around his waist to the end of his life as penance for his sin.

Achievements and talents Like most of his line, he was energetic in his exercise of kingship. He oversaw and extended civil and criminal justice, he brought the Highlands more fully into the kingdom (he was the last Scots king to speak Gaelic), and he travelled extensively around the country, exercising his personal power. James' court, too, was a place of erudition and learning as well as of ceremony and pageantry. He was a great patron of the arts, with men like William **Dunbar** and Robert Carver, the composer, at his court. He was also a lover of architecture, and royal building – for example, at Holyrood, Linlithgow and Stirling – assumed much greater importance in his reign. With his advisers, he was responsible for extending the scope of education in the country, founding a new university at Aberdeen and requiring that the eldest sons of landowners should learn Latin and read the

law. He encouraged the establishment of a printing press in Edinburgh, built up the Scots navy (for the building of which the Scottish forests were stripped bare) and artillery, and never ceased in his personal pursuit of knowledge.

Opinions of others The humanist scholar Erasmus, tutor to one of James' bastard sons, said of the king 'He had a wonderful intellectual power, an astonishing knowledge of everything, and unconquerable magnanimity, and the most abundant generosity.' Other testaments affirm the king's qualities. One of the few negative comments, made by the Spanish ambassador to his own king in an otherwise glowing report of James, was that 'he is not a good captain because he begins to fight before he gives orders' – an observation which proved tragically prophetic.

Relations with women and his marriage As well as being energetic in his exercise of kingship, James was vigorous in his pursuit of women – at least before his marriage – and probably had at least seven illegitimate children by the time he was 25. In 1503 he married Margaret Tudor, daughter of Henry VII of England. The day after their first, formal meeting James paid his bride-to-be a more informal visit, and to show her accomplishment she danced while James played the harpsichord and lute. He rounded off his visit by showing off in front of Margaret, jumping up onto his horse without the aid of a stirrup. Of the couple's six children, only one, the future **James V**, survived to adulthood.

War with England and Flodden James' marriage to a Tudor ultimately allowed his great-grandson, **James VI**, to accede to the throne of England a century later. For James himself, however, it brought a complication to his foreign policy, with the 'Treaty of Perpetual Peace' agreed between Scotland and England before the marriage. Scotland had always been allied to France rather than England, the traditional enemy. When war broke out between France and England, the pull of the 'Auld Alliance' was stronger than that of the new, and James determined to invade England in support of the French. Just before his departure, he is said to have seen at Linlithgow a spectre who warned him to abandon the venture (although the whole episode may have been set up by David **Lyndsay**). In any event, he would have been wiser to take the advice. Although brave, he was no general, and basic blunders of tactics and strategy against the English force left James and many of his nobles dead in the mud at Flodden on 9 September 1513. The new king, James V, was a 17-month-old baby. With stormy winds of change blowing in from the Continent, a long period of minority rule was the last thing Scotland needed, and the futile disaster of Flodden was a near-mortal blow from which the country never fully recovered.

James V
1512–1542
King of Scots

James was born at Linlithgow and was an infant when he succeeded his father, **James IV**, after the Battle of Flodden in 1513. It was not until 1528 that he was able to begin his personal rule.

Financial and administrative successes James V shared the Stewart traits of efficiency and energy, and was an effective ruler. Like his father, he was a patron of the arts, and carried on the royal building programme. However, he was also avaricious and vindictive. His reign certainly enriched the Crown, and it was thought that he picked off wealthy nobles for forfeiture. He also exploited the break with the papacy made by his English uncle, Henry VIII, to wring as much money as he could from the weakened Church; five of his bastard sons were foisted on the Church, appointed to high office while still children.

His marriages In 1536 he travelled to France to marry the Duke of Vendôme's daughter but changed his mind after visiting her, disguised as a servant. He went on to the court of the French king where he fell in love with the king's daughter, Madeleine. The two were married in 1537, but James' happiness was short-lived, as Madeleine died a few months later. Her death saw the introduction of mourning dress into Scotland for the first time. In 1538 he married Mary of Guise. Tragically, the couple's first children, two sons, died within a month of one another in 1541.

Final days Relations with England deteriorated into war in 1542. Mindful of Flodden and resentful of James, the nobles were reluctant to join, resulting in a rout of the Scots at Solway Moss. James' health, already strained, was broken by the defeat, and on hearing that his wife had given birth to a daughter, **Mary**, he reflected on his family's royal succession with the words, 'It cam' wi' a lass and it will pass wi' a lass'. He died six days after her birth.

James VI
1566–1625
King of Scots

Learned, moderate, vigorous and possessed of a first-class mind, James VI has stood the tests of history to emerge as one of the most successful of all Scottish monarchs.

Bleak early years He was the son of Queen **Mary** and her second husband, **Darnley**, and was born at Edinburgh Castle on 19 June 1566. James' reign began inauspiciously after the effective deposition of his mother in 1567. As with many of his predecessors, his minority years were marred by factional in-fighting among the nobility, but now with the ambitious and dangerous aspirations of the reformed Church of Scotland added to the political mix. Unlike his predecessors, however, James grew up with no parental affection to fall back on; in fact, his childhood, dominated by the nightmarish figure of his tutor, George **Buchanan**, seems to have been unusually harsh in that respect.

Routing of nobility and Church James began to assert his personal authority around 1584. How dangerous the cocktail of ambitious nobility and extreme Protestantism could be had been brought home forcibly to James in 1582 in what became known as the Ruthven Raid, when he was effectively kidnapped by a group of extremist nobles intent on gaining power for themselves. Crushing overweening nobles was not difficult, but the claims of the Church were a serious threat to royal power, and the king dealt with them from the 1590s onwards. Ambitious ministers claimed their right to intervene in politics while denying the king any say in the running of the Church. By means of manipulation of the General Assembly, the Church's ruling body, judicious appointments of moderates to posts of power and, later, the imposition of bishops into a presbyterian church, James skilfully won out, proving himself in the process a most shrewd political operator.

Administrative successes
By the end of the 16th century, the king controlled the country more effectively, and in return for less physical effort, than any of his royal predecessors. Government control now stretched into every corner of the land, including the Highlands. This state of affairs enabled James in later years to make his famous claim that he ruled Scotland more effectively with his pen than his ancestors had done with the sword.

His writings Like almost all the Stewart monarchs, James was a patron of the arts, but unlike the others he was also an author in his own right, displaying his learning and intelligence in a series of books on various topics published throughout his reign. It was the claims of the Church of Scotland to effective political power which led him to expound his ideas on the divine right of kings to rule in the work *The Trew Law of Free Monarchies*. This was simply a justification of the monarch's place, over the Church or any other challenger, as supreme political power in the land. Also among his most famous works is *Demonologie*. Published in 1599, it both sprang from and fed the fear of witchcraft sweeping Europe at the time. (Such was James' preoccupation with the topic that in 1605 Shakespeare wrote *Macbeth* especially to please the king.) James was probably also the first anti-smoker to express his views in print: his *Counterblaste to Tobacco* declares smoking 'A custome lothsome to the eye, hatefull to the Nose, harmefull to the braine, dangerous to the lungs, and in the black stinking fume thereof, neerest resembling the horrible Stigian smoake of the pit that is bottomlesse.'

Marriage and family In 1589 James married Princess Anne of Denmark. The two enjoyed a reasonably happy marriage and had seven children, four of whom died in infancy. Prince Henry, the couple's bright, outgoing eldest son, for whom James had written his practical guide to kingship, *Basilikon Doron*, died in 1612 at 18 years of age. His death was devastating to both his parents, but especially to his mother, who largely retired from court to her room for several months on end. The succession now fell to Henry's more introspective younger brother, James and Anne's second son, the future and ill-fated Charles I.

King of Scotland and England In 1603 James, King of Scots, also became king of England on the death of his mother's cousin, Elizabeth I. His accession was not accompanied by the political union which was James' fondest desire, the notion of which was unpopular in both countries. While James' reign as king of Scots alone was outstandingly successful, he lost some of his political judgement after several years in England. He continued to rule Scotland with skill, but in his capacity as king of England his policy in Ireland has emerged as a disastrous one. The Plantation of Ulster, an apparent solution to the problem of a country which wanted freedom from English rule, added a complicating factor which itself has now grown into one of the most intractable political and social problems in the world.

In keeping with his life as a highly able politician and administrator rather than a warrior, James was one of the few Scots kings to die at peace and in his bed.

John Paul Jones
1747–1792
Hero of the War of American Independence

Early life in Scotland and America John Paul, as he began life, was born a gardener's son at Kirkbean in Kirkcudbrightshire. He was apprenticed as a sailor at 12 years of age and worked on a slave ship, in smuggling and in trading across the Atlantic for 15 years. In 1773 he inherited property in Virginia and in 1775, at the start of the War of American Independence he joined the American navy under the assumed name of Jones.

Naval guerrilla tactics After some daring skirmishes in US waters he came to Europe in 1778 in the USS *Ranger*, harrying British ships in the Irish Sea and landing at the port of Whitehaven. He spiked the guns of the fort there and only narrowly missed burning a 300-strong fleet berthed in the harbour. Crossing over to Ireland, Jones captured the British sloop-of-war Drake at Carrickfergus and took the ship to Brest.

The following year, in the USS *Bonhomme Richard*, he terrorised east coast ports from Leith southwards. He encountered the much larger HMS *Serapis* off Flamborough Head and captured her in an action that reads like a boy's-own tale of derring-do. Standing on the deck of his blazing ship, Jones refused the British commander's call to surrender by shouting, 'I have not yet begun to fight!' He managed to lash the two ships together and with a well-aimed grenade destroyed the enemy ammunition and powder supplies, killing many British sailors in the process.

Service in Russia Jones spent several years in the service of the French navy before moving on to Russia in 1788, where Catherine the Great made him a rear-admiral. He played a distinguished part in the Battle of Liman against the Turks that year, but quarrelled with Russian marshal Potemkin and left the country. He died in Paris of dropsy and liver disease in 1792.

Captain Kidd
c. 1645–1701
Pirate, adventurer and merchant

Professional life Other than that he was born in Greenock and was the son of a minister, not much is known of William Kidd's early life. By the 1680s he was settled in America and lived in New York, where he married. He was a sea captain and owned at least one ship which traded in the West Indies.

Privateering commission In the war between England and France in the 1690s, Kidd rose to prominence as a privateer who successfully defended American and English trade routes with the West Indies. As a result of his success he was commissioned by the English government to take charge of an expedition against pirates in the Indian Ocean, and set off early in 1697.

Double-dealing and betrayal By 1698–99 word reached London that, rather than raiding enemy ships, Kidd had himself turned pirate and was preying on the ships of friendly countries. He stayed in the area for two years, finally capturing the rich *Queda Merchant* and her cargo worth £70,000, and setting sail for the West Indies. On his arrival in Hispaniola (now Haiti and the Dominican Republic) in 1699, he discovered that he had been proclaimed pirate in his absence. The English authorities offered him a pardon in return for his surrender, and he set off in another ship for Boston. However, he was dealt with treacherously, and was carted off to London as a prisoner.

Execution He was found guilty at the Old Bailey in a shamelessly rigged trial with very little hard evidence, of the murder of a crewman and of piracy. Kidd's defence, that his men mutinied and that he had no alternative but to go along, was not accepted and he was hanged at Wapping. He never revealed the whereabouts of the *Queda Merchant* or her cargo, which was popularly assumed to have been buried on a remote 'treasure' island.

John Knox
c. 1513–1572
Protestant reformer

Place in history John Knox is one of the most famous religious reformers of the 16th century, and a man who played an important part in the turbulent history of Scotland at that time.

Early religious conviction Born at Haddington around 1513, he studied briefly at university before going on to practice law and enter into minor orders. Little is known of his life until 1544, by when he was a tutor in East Lothian and already a Lutheran. His support of the murder of Cardinal Beaton in 1646 led to his imprisonment for 18 months on a French galley.

Influence of Geneva On his release in 1549 he travelled to England where he gained favour at the court of the Protestant Edward VI. However, the young king's death in 1553 and the accession of his Catholic sister, Mary, drew Knox away to the Continent. In the next few years he travelled between France, Scotland, Germany and, most notably, Geneva, where he was influenced by the ideas of the reformer Calvin.

The Monstrous Regiment In 1558 he published his famous *First Blast of the Trumpet Against the Monstrous Regiment of Women*, directed particularly against the Regent, Mary of Guise, widow of **James V**, and the English Queen Mary. In it, Knox declared that 'to promote a woman to bear rule, superiority, dominion or empire above any realm is repugnant to nature, contrary to God, and … is the subversion of good order, of all equity and justice.' But his tirade backfired, not only when many of his natural allies, including Calvin, distanced themselves from him but, most spectacularly, when Queen Elizabeth acceded to the English throne in 1559. Not surprisingly, she took the criticisms personally, and refused to allow Knox to set foot in her realm.

Reformation in Scotland In 1559 he returned to Scotland where

reformed ideas were gaining ground. Open religious civil war threatened, but the death of the regent in 1560 let Parliament open the way for Protestantism, in drawing up the Confession of Faith, setting out the Calvinist doctrines of the new Church of Scotland, and the First Book of Discipline, establishing presbyterianism as the form of church government, with attendant forms of worship and discipline. Knox, one of the foremost ministers in the country with the parish of St Giles', was influential in drawing up both. He was not a theologian, and was most concerned with the practical application of religion to society, which he now realised in the new church discipline.

Relationship with Mary 1561 saw the return to Scotland of the Catholic Queen **Mary** after the death of her first husband. The politically vulnerable queen could not move against Knox. His attitude to her was one of outright hostility, and the two had several interviews during which he chastised her for her religion, her marriage to **Darnley**, and her conduct, including her fondness for dancing. The disrespect with which he addressed her moved Mary to tears of anger on at least one occasion.

Relations with women Knox himself married at this time. His first marriage, in 1553, had been a cause of scurrilous gossip: one of his correspondents in Berwick had given him the hand in marriage of her second-youngest daughter, a girl considerably younger than Knox was. The girl's mother had then left her husband to accompany her new son-in-law and her daughter to Geneva, and stayed with them for several years. The couple had had two sons, but his wife died in 1560. In 1564 Knox's second marriage was also unusual. His new wife was a Stewart noblewoman (a fact which outraged the queen) who, at barely 16, was at least 35 years his junior. They had three daughters.

Personality revealed in writings and work Knox died from a stroke in 1572. His major work in his final years was the writing of his *History of the Reformation in Scotland*. This is one of the few narrative documents of the time, and with his tendency to emphasise his own place in events, it is sometimes difficult to tell if Knox deserves quite all the credit he has acquired as the only leading light in the Scottish Reformation.

Knox was utterly convinced of his own salvation and of the damnation of those who disagreed with him, and equated his own will with the will of God. His writings reveal a man capable of insight and humour, but of a type which was often spiteful and emerged only in his views of his opponents. His dogmatic and dictatorial personality, combined with the bleak and joyless rigour of the system of church discipline he bequeathed to the country, make him a man whom it is difficult to like. His courage, however, cannot be faulted.

Robert Knox
1791–1862
Anatomist

Distinguished career and marriage Robert Knox was the eighth child of an Edinburgh maths teacher. As a child he contracted smallpox which left him blind in one eye and scarred but these setbacks did not deter his scholastic brilliance both at school and Edinburgh University, from which he graduated as a physician in 1814. After five years as an army doctor, when he served at Waterloo and in the Cape, he returned to Edinburgh, and by 1826 he was head of his own anatomy school. He married, in what appears to have been a love match, a working-class woman; his choice of wife was said to have damaged his career prospects. Of Knox's six children, only one survived him.

Association with Burke and Hare Knox was a skilled anatomist and an outstanding lecturer; his lectures were events, for which he took the trouble to dress up, and they attracted over 500 students at a time. His success and high profile meant that he was a market for the gruesome peddlars of Edinburgh's flourishing 'resurrection' trade. Unfortunately for Knox, in 1827–28 he also became a customer of **Burke and Hare**, who murdered to gain their corpses, rather than dig them out of the ground. The murderers cleared Knox of knowledge of the crimes, but he was condemned and burnt in effigy. A committee of his peers cleared him of complicity but left doubt as to his knowledge of events.

Later career In the 1830s his school's popularity waned, and he failed to gain professorships at Edinburgh and Aberdeen. In 1856 he took up a post as pathological anatomist at the Cancer Hospital at Brompton in London. He was honoured by several institutions in the following years, and died in the city in 1862. Bridie's play *The Anatomist* and **Stevenson**'s horror story *The Body Snatcher*, are both based on Knox's life.

Harry Lauder
1870–1950
Entertainer

Childhood singer Harry Lauder was born in Portobello, the eldest of eight children of a potter. His father died when he was 12 and his mother took the children to Arbroath where she had relatives. While still at school, Harry worked as a flax spinner in a local mill and entered talent and singing competitions.

Turning professional At the age of 14 Harry moved to Hamilton at his uncle's suggestion, to work in the Lanarkshire coal mines. He gained a name for himself locally as he travelled around, entering and winning local talent competitions. He gradually gained fame in professional circles in Glasgow, and in 1900 he moved to London, where he was an almost immediate success. His popularity grew: the bekilted, singing, Scotch caricature was popular inside Scotland as well as outside, and he achieved phenomenal success worldwide.

Personal tragedy While Lauder was living in Lanarkshire he had met and married the daughter of his pit manager, but the couple were devastated when their only son was killed in the First World War. The song *Keep Right on to the End of the Road* was written after the tragedy. Although he continued to perform – especially for the troops at the front, receiving a knighthood for his efforts – he never fully recovered from the blow.

Enduring success Lauder's success was based on talent and hard work; he would rehearse one song every day, often for weeks at a time, to make sure it was exactly right. He wrote some of the most famous Scots songs, including *Stop Yer Ticklin', Jock*, *Roamin' in the Gloamin'* and *I Love a Lassie* (written by his wife). He came to represent Scotland and all things Scottish for millions, and although his caricature Scot is resented by many in Scotland today, he remains the most famous of Scottish entertainers.

Eric Liddell
1902–1945
Athlete and missionary

Background and sporting skills Eric Henry Liddell was born in China, one of four children of a missionary, and came to Scotland when he was five years old. Liddell made a name for himself as a runner at school and at Edinburgh University, excelling at sprint and middle distance and acquiring the nickname 'The Flying Scotsman'. He was also picked to play rugby for Scotland.

Sabbatarianism and Olympic gold Liddell was chosen to go with the British team to the 1924 Paris Olympic Games, where he was entered for the 100 and 200 metres sprints. However, he withdrew from the 100 metres competition because the heats were to be run on a Sunday, something which his Sabbatarian views could not countenance. He went on to take the bronze medal in the 200 metres. He also entered the 400 metres, an event in which he was inexperienced; sensationally, he took the gold medal with a new world record. (Liddell's story, and that of Harold Abrahams, the victor in the 100 metres, was told in the 1981 film, *Chariots of Fire*.) Liddell went on to cap a spectacular year by graduating from Edinburgh University a few days later.

Missionary life and death Liddell decided on a missionary life and spent the following year studying divinity. In 1925 took up a post in the Anglo-Chinese College in Tientsin, where he continued his running. He came back to Scotland to be ordained a minister in 1931, and in 1934 he married Florence McKenzie, a Canadian nurse. The couple returned to China, but in 1941, after the Japanese invasion, Liddell sent away his pregnant wife and two young daughters to safety. He never saw his new third baby daughter. He continued to work in China, and in 1943 he and his fellow missionaries were interned in a Japanese camp at Weifeng, where he died of a brain tumour in February 1945.

Robert Liston
1794–1847
Surgeon and pioneer of anaesthetics

Medical training Robert Liston, the son of a minister, was born in Linlithgow. He was educated mainly by his father before going to Edinburgh University to study medicine in 1808. One of his main teachers there was the anatomist John Barclay, who had also been the mentor of Robert **Knox** and who inspired Liston's interest in anatomy and surgery. He graduated in 1814 and took up a post as a house officer at the Royal Infirmary in Edinburgh for two years. He spent some time in London, then returned to Edinburgh as a teacher of anatomy and a surgeon.

Surgical skills In the time before the use of anaesthetics, speed, skill and accuracy were critically important in operations, and Liston had all in abundance. It was said that 'the gleam of his knife was followed so instantaneously by the sound of sawing as to make the two actions appear almost simultaneous'. He could conclude difficult operations in seconds, and was renowned particularly for his skill in amputations. He took on and successfully concluded work which other surgeons had turned down, and his reputation extended throughout Europe and America. However, he made many enemies in Edinburgh by quarrelling with the authorities at the Royal Infirmary, and in 1833 he failed to gain the professorship of Clinical Surgery. In 1834 he took a post as surgeon at the new University College Hospital in London, becoming Professor of Clinical Surgery there the following year. Liston died of an aneurysm – ironically, one of his specialties – at his home in London in 1847.

Advances in anaesthetics Liston made history when he became the first to use a general anaesthetic in a public operation in London in 1846. He also gave his name to the Liston Splint, the treatment he devised for dislocation of the thigh.

David Livingstone
1813–1873
Missionary and explorer

David Livingstone – doctor, missionary and one of the first to explore the Dark Continent – was a 19th-century hero.

Training for Africa The son of a Blantyre shopkeeper, David worked in a mill from the age of 10. Despite personal hardship, he educated himself in his spare time after the long working days in the mill. He attended Anderson's College and Glasgow University, studying medicine and theology to enable him to work as a missionary doctor. In 1840, after a year's training with the London Missionary Society, he got his first posting in Africa.

Missionary doctor In 1841 Livingstone arrived at the mission at Bechuanaland run by Robert Moffat, another Scot; three years later he married Moffat's daughter, Mary. Bechuanaland was his base for the next few years, although his work doctoring and seeking native assistants to help him in his conversions took him far into areas which were relatively uncharted.

Zambezi and the Victoria Falls In 1849 Livingstone joined the English explorer William Oswell in his search for Lake Ngami. Their success won them great fame at home, but the hardships of Africa took their toll on the health of Livingstone's family. His wife was ill – she had already lost one child – and in 1852 she returned to Britain with their four children (the rigours she endured finally killed her in 1862). Livingstone now pressed further into western central Africa, mapping the upper Zambezi River and, most famously, discovering the Victoria Falls in 1855. At the end 1856 he came home to a hero's welcome.

Another expedition and the slave trade Livingstone's missionary work was now taking second place to his exploration, and he resigned from the London Missionary Society. By 1558 he was back in Africa, this time at the head of a government expedition

to explore the Zambezi. Mapping the terrain of Africa was important for its own sake and for the economic aspirations of the imperial powers. But this trip, hampered by mismanagement and the operations of the Portuguese slave traders, was a relative failure, and it was called home in 1863. However, the trip had exposed Livingstone to the full horrors of the slave trade, and his *Zambesi and its Tributaries*, published in 1864, was influential in the ending of the trade. (His ideals were also shared by his son, who died fighting for the Union in the American Civil War.)

'Dr Livingstone, I presume?' In 1865, at the request of the Royal Geographical Society, Livingstone set out on his last trip in search of the source of the Nile. His expedition headed west from Zanzibar to Ujiji. Again, the problems were great: Livingstone almost died several times from disease; his medicines were lost; and much of his supplies were stolen. From Ujiji he headed up what he mistakenly thought was a Nile tributary, but fell ill and was forced to return. He had been unheard of in the west for years, and the reporter H. M. Stanley of the *New York Herald* had been sent by his editor to find Livingstone. He caught up with him at Ujiji, and Stanley's first words of greeting, 'Dr Livingstone, I presume?', have passed into history. But Stanley could not persuade Livingstone to leave Africa and the explorer died the following year. His attendants embalmed his body and brought it back for burial in Westminster Abbey.

Robert Lorimer
1864–1929
Architect

Apprenticeship Robert Lorimer was born in Edinburgh, the son of one of Scotland's most distinguished lawyers. He was educated at Edinburgh University, but after three years' study he left in 1885 without a degree. He became apprentice in one of the foremost architects' offices in Edinburgh at the time, going on to London in 1889 to widen his experience. In 1892 he returned to Edinburgh to set up his own practice.

Development of his style It may have been during his time in London that Lorimer was attracted by the ideas of the Arts and Crafts movement, with their emphasis on traditional forms, construction and craftsmanship. Lorimer took the principles of Arts and Crafts and modified and adapted them to traditional Scottish architectural forms, such as Scots Baronial. The resulting buildings ranged from country houses, such as the remodelled Rowallan Castle in Ayrshire, to rows of colonies cottages for craftsmen in Edinburgh. The resulting architecture was, along with the more revolutionary work of Charles Rennie **Mackintosh** in Glasgow, the first distinctively Scottish style to emerge for over a century.

His work Lorimer worked in other architectural styles, including Gothic and classical. He was highly successful, attracting commissions from across the country. Most of these were private houses and castles, but he was also interested in garden design, and redesigned the gardens at, for example, Balmanno Castle in Perthshire. Two of Lorimer's most famous public works are in Edinburgh: in the Thistle Chapel in St Giles' Cathedral, and the National War Memorial at the Castle, completed in 1928. Lorimer was knighted in 1911 and died in 1929.

David Lyndsay
c. 1486–1555
Poet and playwright

David Lyndsay was born at either his father's house of the Mount near Cupar, or at Garmylton near Haddington. He is thought to have attended St Andrews University and was employed at the court of **James IV** in 1508.

Infant royal favour In 1512 he was appointed usher to the baby prince, the future **James V**. The post, which he held for 10 years, involved mostly playing with James, carrying him around, singing to him and amusing him by acting out his favourite fairy tales or dressing up as a ghost. He was also believed to have been responsible for the appearance of another 'ghost', this time at Linlithgow Palace in 1513, warning James IV against his fateful invasion of England. In 1522 Lyndsay married Janet Douglas, the king's seamstress. He fell briefly from favour during the royal minority but when James began exercising his authority Lyndsay became Lyon King of Arms, the head of the College of Heralds, receiving a knighthood in the process, and effective court poet.

His work and views Lyndsay began writing in his late 30s with his first poem, *The Dreme*. His style is vigorous, with an earthy humour and vividness. His work entertained and advised: he satirised the vices of court life and even rebuked the king for his licentious behaviour and his susceptibility to flattery – for example in *The Testament and Complaynt of our Soverane Lordis Papyngo*, where the king's pet parrot criticises court, clergy and nobility – yet he remained one of James' favourites. He also satirised the failings of the Church, and is believed to have encouraged Knox to preach. Lyndsay's views are amply demonstrated in his 1540 masterpiece, *Ane Pleasant Satyre of the Thrie Estatis*, a morality play which is still performed today. Despite his sympathy for the reformers, Lyndsay died a Catholic.

John Loudon McAdam
1756–1836
Road builder

American exile and return John Loudon McAdam was born in Ayr, the youngest of 10 children. When his father died in 1770 he was sent to his uncle in New York where he made money working in a counting-house. On the outbreak of war in 1775 he joined a loyalist regiment with the result that he lost money after the war ended. He returned to Scotland with his American family in 1783 with enough money to buy an estate in Ayrshire.

Road construction system On his new estate McAdam experimented with ideas he had for road construction. Roads were notoriously bad – dusty, rutted tracks in dry weather, morasses of mud in the wet. McAdam devised a construction of stones, largest at the bottom and smallest at the surface, laid on drained soil and with a camber to allow drainage. His revolutionary roads were inexpensive, flexible, almost waterproof and silent.

On the road In 1798 McAdam took up an administrative post in the Navy and moved to Falmouth. But he continued his experiments and in the next 16 years spent £5,000 of his own money and 2,000 days travelling around 30,000 miles, researching and inspecting Britain's roads. In 1815 he gained his first professional appointment, as surveyor-general of Bristol roads. His system was now gaining wide acceptance, and in 1827 he was appointed general surveyor of roads by Parliament, receiving some recompense for his past expenditure.

Significance In the time before the railways McAdam's roads were vital for moving people and goods around the industrialising country, and the philosopher Jeremy Bentham declared that 'McAdam's system justified the perpetuation of McAdam's name in popular speech'. The terms 'macadamised' and 'macadamisation' were used to describe the new roads and their building.

Macbeth
c. 1005–1057
King of Scots

Shakespeare's version Macbeth owes his prominence in Scottish history not to any achievements of his own reign but to his role as arch-villain in one of the greatest of William Shakespeare's plays. Shakespeare's account was based, at third or fourth hand, on the historian Hector Boece's *Latin History of Scotland*, and drew from it various stories, including Macbeth's and Banquo's meeting with the witches; the ambition of Gruoch, Macbeth's wife; the murders first of Duncan, then of Banquo; and the final battle at Dunsinane in which Macbeth was defeated. These myths and fictional accounts have assumed a greater credence – and indeed interest – than the prosaic reality of the story of a reasonably successful early-medieval monarch.

Succession battles Macbeth was one of at least two claimants to the Scots throne after the death in 1034 of Malcolm II, who had no sons. Macbeth was Mormaer of Moray, one of the Pictish earldoms, and was of royal blood himself. His wife, Gruoch, as a granddaughter of Kenneth II, was also of the royal line. But the throne passed to Duncan, Malcolm's grandson. In 1040 Macbeth met Duncan in battle and defeated and killed him. Duncan's sons, Malcolm and Donald Bán, fled to England for safety.

His reign Not a great deal is known of Macbeth's reign, although the country was relatively stable under his government. The king was a benefactor of the Church and was confident enough in his own rule and the security of his kingdom to be able to leave Scotland and travel to Rome on pilgrimage in 1050, when he is said to have 'scattered alms like seed corn'. He was finally defeated in battle by Malcolm at Lumphanan in Aberdeenshire in 1057. He had no children. He is buried on the Hebridean island of Iona.

Hugh MacDiarmid
1892–1978
Poet

Education and early career Hugh MacDiarmid was the pseudonym of Christopher Murray Grieve. He was born in Langholm, the elder son of a postman. He attended the local school and he was a voracious reader, later claiming to have read all the books in the local library. He abandoned teacher-training in favour of journalism, and during the First World War he saw service as a sergeant in the Royal Army Medical Corps.

Poetry After the war MacDiarmid lived in Montrose, working for the *Review*, a local paper. The first work of poetry he published at this time was written in English, but his imagination was fired by a Scots dictionary from the town library, and he used words from different dialects to build up a literary Scots language. In 1926 he published his best-known work, *A Drunk Man Looks at the Thistle*, a self-parodic poem of meditation and introspection. In the 1930s MacDiarmid spent eight years living in poverty on the Shetland island of Whalsay; his first marriage had ended, and his mental health was not good. By now he was backing away from the exclusive use of Scots in his work, and the material he published during this period, such as *Stony Limits and Other Poems*, is acknowledged as among his best.

Political beliefs Politics played an important part in his life. His father was a radical, while he himself worked for the ILP and Fabian Research Department. He helped found the SNP, from which he was later expelled, and he joined the Communist Party twice, with a 19-year period of expulsion between memberships.

His work MacDiarmid's later work never achieved the quality of which he had shown himself capable. Though his concerns changed through his life, he was always a philosophical poet, an intellectual to whom ideas were real.

Flora Macdonald
1725–1789
Jacobite heroine

Traumatic early life Flora Macdonald was born at Milton in South Uist where her father was a tacksman, or manager-farmer, of Clanranald. He died when she was only two years old, and at six she also lost her mother, who was abducted and married by Hugh Macdonald of Skye. Flora stayed with her brother, Angus, until she was 13, when she was taken into the home of the Clanranald chiefs to be educated. In 1739 she went to live with Sir Alexander Macdonald of the Isles and his wife, Margaret, at Monkstadt on Skye, staying with them for several years.

Flight from Benbecula to Skye It was in 1746 on a return visit to the Clanranald home on Benbecula that she was asked to help Prince **Charles** Edward Stuart, fugitive after Culloden with a price of £30,000 on his head. The prince was to cross from Benbecula to Skye, and Flora agreed to help, although she was not happy that he was to be dressed as a woman. He was listed on Flora's papers as 'Betty Burke, an Irish spinning-maid'. It was known that the prince was in the area, and Government militia were monitoring all movements around the coast. The boat party was fired on by militia on Skye, but managed to land. Flora sought help from Lady Macdonald in Monkstadt. She hid the party in a nearby cottage that night, and the next day Flora took the prince to Portree, whence he sailed to Raasay. As a final gift Charles gave Flora a golden locket containing his portrait, and took his leave with the words, 'I hope, madam, that we may meet in St James' yet.' Flora never saw the prince again.

Imprisonment The boatmen were arrested on their return to Benbecula, and confessed all. Flora was arrested and imprisoned in the Tower of London until the Jacobite amnesty of 1747.

Marriage She returned to the islands and in 1750 married a kins-

man, Allan Macdonald of Kingsburgh in Skye; they had nine children, two of whom died in infancy. In 1773 she met and entertained Dr Samuel Johnson during his tour with **Boswell**; Johnson described her as 'a woman of soft features, elegant manners and gentle presence'. The following year Flora and her family, beset by debt, emigrated to North Carolina.

Return from America

It was an inauspicious time to move to America, and after the outbreak of the revolutionary war Allan was made a brigadier-general in the loyalist forces by the governor. Flora accompanied him until he was taken prisoner by the rebels. In 1779, on her husband's advice, Flora set sail again for Scotland. Her ship was attacked during the crossing by a French privateer, although she insisted on remaining on deck, and suffered a broken arm during the skirmish. She lived in a cottage near her brother until her husband's return two years later, when they moved back to Kingsburgh.

Death and burial   When Flora died there in 1790 she was wrapped in the sheet in which both Charles and Johnson had slept, and was buried in the local churchyard at Kilmuir. An obelisk, paid for by donations, was erected in her memory after the grave's original headstone was gradually chipped away and carried off by innumerable over-enthusiastic souvenir hunters.

John Macdonald
1815–91
Canadian statesman

Emigration   When John Macdonald was five years old his father took the family from Glasgow to settle in Kingston in Upper Canada (now Ontario). John attended the local school and at 15 began a six-year apprenticeship with a Kingston lawyer. He was admitted to the bar in 1836 and the practice he set up became one of the most successful in Canada.

Political career   In 1844 he was elected Conservative representative for Kingston to the House of Assembly, a joint body administering Upper and Lower Canada (Quebec). His energy won him a place in the cabinet in three years. In 1854 he was made attorney-general in a new Conservative administration. He had been the party's leading light for some time, and on the resignation in 1857 of the premier, Colonel Tache, Macdonald became both leader of the Conservatives and premier.

Expansion of Canada   Canada on Macdonald's death in 1891 was unrecognisable from the country he took over in 1857. Largely through his influence, Nova Scotia and New Brunswick had entered the new Dominion in 1867, to be joined by Manitoba, British Columbia and Prince Edward Island in the 1870s, and including the North West Territories, with the capital in Ottawa. He also secured the construction of the Canadian Pacific railroad, an enterprise vital in a country so vast.

Loyalist   By the time of Macdonald's death he was regarded as the foremost statesman in North America. Throughout the whole of his 47 years in politics his basic opinions never wavered: pro-confederation, anti-American and conservative, his greatest ambition was 'to be a subject of a great British-American nation, under the government of her majesty, and in connection with the empire of Great Britain and Ireland.'

Ramsay MacDonald
1866–1937
First Labour Prime Minister

Poor beginnings The illegitimate son of a Lossiemouth servant, Ramsay MacDonald came from desperately poor beginnings. He attended local school before spending several years moving between his home and London, seeking employment and educating himself. The grinding poverty he endured in his search for work reduced him at times to eating oatmeal, sent from home by his mother, mixed with cold water. His reading, coupled with his own experiences, reinforced his belief in the need for social reform through parliamentary means.

Electoral success His first political break came in 1886 when he became private secretary to a Gladstonian parliamentary candidate. By now he was a member of the Fabian Society of left-wing intellectuals (who never trusted him throughout their long association), and in 1893 he joined Keir **Hardie**'s new ILP. In 1900 he helped bring the trade unions into their new Labour Party, and in the 1906 General Election he was one of the 29 new Labour MPs returned. MacDonald was party secretary for 11 years, and in 1911 became leader. In this year he suffered his greatest personal blow in the death of his wife, Margaret. They had been married for 15 years and MacDonald, a somewhat solitary figure, had blossomed under his gregarious wife's influence. Five of their six children survived to adulthood.

War and political isolation MacDonald felt even more solitary during the war, when his stand made him the most hated public figure in the country. He opposed the war, but when Britain joined he considered speedy victory a moral imperative, while abhorring jingoism and calling for moderation in shaping the peace treaty with Germany. He also welcomed Kerensky's liberal revolution in Russia. He was denounced as a traitor, and lost first the party leadership then his seat. But his true talents lay in foreign affairs: his stand on the war and the revolution in Russia, his support for the League of Nations, his attempts to co-operate with the Russians, Germans and French in the 1920s, and his active interest in reconciling the Indian Hindu and Muslim communities all now seem more far-sighted than was then realised.

A Labour Government

By 1923 he was back in Parliament at the head of his party, and in 1924 he was leader of the first, minority, Labour Government. Although Prime Minister for only nine months, his administration proved Labour's ability to govern.

National Government and political suicide

In 1929 he was PM again but found himself riding the whirlwind of world recession which saw unemployment in Britain jump from one to three million in two years and the pound plummet. The cabinet could not agree on the handling of the crisis, and MacDonald offered the Government's resignation; instead, he was persuaded by the king to remain as the head of a 'National' Government drawn from all parties. To MacDonald this was a short-term expedient to deal with a critical situation, but the length of the recession, coupled with the bitterness of betrayal felt by his former colleagues, made the breach with his party permanent. No longer Labour leader but still PM, he eventually resigned in 1935. Two years later, his health broken by the strain, he was dead.

William MacEwen
1848–1924
Pioneer of neurosurgery

Early influences   William MacEwen was the youngest son of a
Rothesay marine trader. He was educated at Glasgow University,
graduating in medicine in 1869. While at Glasgow MacEwen
encountered the university's pioneering professor of surgery,
Joseph Lister, then gaining recognition for his use of antisepsis in
surgical operations. MacEwen became a convert to Lister's methods, and after his appointment as assistant surgeon at the Royal
Infirmary in Glasgow in 1875, he abandoned his other medical
interests to concentrate entirely on surgery.

Neurosurgical and other advances   MacEwen was a single-mind-
ed and self-confident surgeon whose methods were based on his
own observations and experience rather than on received information. He used Lister's advances to take surgery into untried
areas and became the first dedicated neurosurgeon. In the late
1870s he scored a string of ground-breaking successes in the diagnosis and treatment of brain disorders: he removed a brain
tumour; he operated to relieve a brain haemorrhage; and he identified middle-ear disease as the commonest cause of brain abscess-
es. But his success was not confined to neurosurgery: he devised
new operations to cure knock-knees and hernias; he performed
successful chest operations, proving that such techniques could be
used without danger to the lungs; and he devised a method of
implanting grafts to replace missing portions of limb bones. This
last advance also allowed him to work as advisor to a group making artificial limbs for the disabled of the First World War.

Recognition of his contributions   MacEwen was appointed to
Lister's former post of Regius Professor of Surgery at Glasgow
University, and after his old teacher's death in 1912 was recog-
nised as the foremost surgeon in Britain.

William McGonagall
c. 1825–1902
Poet

Family background William McGonagall was the son of an Irish weaver, and was born probably in Edinburgh. The family moved to South Ronaldsay in Orkney until William was 11 years old, when they settled in Dundee. He followed his father into the weaving industry.

His poetry McGonagall was something of a showman, and loved to perform in amateur dramatics on stage in Dundee. It was presumably this desire to perform which drew him into writing poetry which was also meant to be dramatic. His subject matter chronicled contemporary events, such as in *The Tay Bridge Disaster*: 'Beautiful Railway Bridge of the Silv'ry Tay! / Alas, I am very sorry to say / That ninety lives have been taken away / On the last Sabbath day of 1879, / Which will be remember'd for a very long time.'; or *The Death of Lord and Lady Dalhousie*: 'Alas! Lord and Lady Dalhousie are dead, and buried at last, / Which causes many people to feel a little downcast.'

Publications and readings A local newspaper printed some of McGonagall's poems, and this encouraged him to have sheets of them printed up which he then sold across central Scotland. He also combined his love of the stage with his poetry, and gave readings in theatres, often waving a sword to make a dramatic point. He good-naturedly put up with barracking from audiences, apparently convinced of his own talent.

His appeal While it is easy to smile at the simplicity of his subject matter, his utter disregard for metre and the sheer badness of his poetry, it has its own appeal and charm. It is not surprising that he has attracted a cult following which has persisted from his own lifetime to the present day and, unlike many who could claim to be much less bad, his works are still in print.

Rob Roy Macgregor
1671–1734
Outlaw and adventurer

Background Robert Macgregor acquired his name of 'Roy' early in life because of his thick, dark red curly hair. He was a grazier who raided cattle and took protection money from neighbours to safeguard their herds, but he was not a common brigand: his surviving papers reveal an intelligent and educated man.

A life of outlawry He made enough money to buy land from the Duke of Montrose, but in 1712 he lost money Montrose had lent him for his cattle-dealing. The duke extracted revenge by seizing his house and goods and turning his wife and four young sons out in the middle of winter. Macgregor's neighbour and distant kinsman, the Duke of Argyll, gave him shelter and encouraged him to wage war on Montrose, Argyll's enemy, by stealing his cattle, robbing his factors and attacking his men.

Sheriffmuir Macgregor was a Jacobite, and in the rebellion of 1715 he marched off apparently to join the forces of the deposed Stuarts at Sheriffmuir. But his benefactor, Argyll, was the London Government's most prominent supporter, so he simply sat and watched the spectacle from a nearby hillside. Neither side was happy with his action, but equally neither was alienated.

Later life and luck From 1717 onwards his lawlessness meant he had to live rough in caves and woods. Tales of his exploits, hair's-breadth escapes and Robin Hood-style wealth redistribution are stirring and well worth reading. In 1727 his luck seemed to have run out when he was captured but on the point of being transported to Barbados he received a pardon. He lived the rest of his life in relative peace on his lands at Balquhidder, his only recorded transgression being the fighting of a duel.

This larger-than-life figure was immortalised by Walter **Scott** in his 1818 novel, *Rob Roy*.

Charles Macintosh
1766–1843
Inventor of waterproof materials

Background Charles was the son of George Macintosh, a prominent dyer, and with such a background, it is not surprising that he had an interest in chemistry. It was this interest which was to change the appearance of rainwear and add a new word to the English language.

Chemical advances In 1785 Macintosh began manufacturing ammonium chloride and started work on new dyeing techniques. By the end of the century he had begun the first Scottish alum works. He had also entered into association with Charles **Tennant**, the foremost industrial chemist of his time. The early Industrial Revolution saw a huge expansion in the British textile industry, and new opportunities were created for chemists who could provide dyes and bleaches for the industry. Tennant took out a patent for a new, easily transportable bleaching powder in 1799, although evidence exists which indicates that Macintosh and not Tennant was actually responsible for the powder.

Waterproof fabric Despite his other work during the period, it was the patent he took out in 1823 for his fabric-waterproofing process which has ensured the survival of his name as a household word. In the process, naphtha, a by-product of coal-tar distillation, was used as a solvent for rubber, which was applied to two pieces of cloth which were subsequently pressed together to form the flexible fabric. Its most obvious application, in the form of a rainproof coat, was given the name of its originator by 1836. However, it was some time before the process was refined sufficiently to reduce the fabric's overpoweringly rubbery smell.

Poetic justice Given Scotland's seemingly permanent state of precipitation, it is fitting that this most basic item of rainwear should have been devised by a Scot.

Compton Mackenzie
1883–1972
Writer

Family background A Scot by inclination, emotion and ancestry, Compton Mackenzie was actually born in England. His name originally was Edward Montague Compton, with the last name only being added later by him to emphasise his Scottishness. He was born into a theatrical family, which doubtless helped to emphasise his own flamboyant and extravagant personality.

Early work and talent He was educated at Oxford University and began studying for the Bar, but he abandoned all legal ambitions in 1907 to concentrate on writing his first play, *The Gentleman in Grey*, with *Passionate Elopement*, his first novel, being published four years later. In 1913 he published *Sinister Street*, one of his most famous works which dealt controversially with adolescence. This brought him the acclaim of some of the foremost writers of his day, including Henry James, who called him 'very much the greatest talent of a new generation'.

Later work During the First World War Mackenzie served in the Dardanelles and was director of the secret service in the Aegean. After the war he lived on the island of Capri, but in 1928 he moved to Scotland for the first time, settling on another island, Barra. This was the background for the most famous of his later comedies of Scottish life, *Whisky Galore*, based on the true story of the wartime wrecking of the SS *Politician*. But Mackenzie's output was prolific, and he continued to write serious work: The ambitious, six-volume semi-autobiographical *Four Winds of Love* explored the issues of the modern world, set around the globe. Mackenzie published his own autobiography, *My Life and Times*, in 10 volumes from 1963 to 1971. He was one of the founder members of the SNP in 1928, and received a knighthood in 1952.

Charles Rennie Mackintosh
1868–1928
Architect, designer and artist

Early career and influences Charles Rennie Mackintosh was born in Glasgow, one of 11 children of a police superintendent. From an early age architecture was the only career he wanted, and when he was 16 he went to work as apprentice in an architect's office. There he learned not only the principles of architecture but also furniture making and design, skills which would allow him to create the total environment so characteristic of his work. In 1884 he also began evening classes at the Glasgow School of Art. The associations and friendships which Charles formed there were central in the development not only of his own style but also in those of his fellow-students, an exceptionally talented group of young men and women who initiated the avant-garde design movement which became known as the Glasgow Style.

Examples of his work The 1890s and early 1900s were Mackintosh's most fruitful, in terms of his architecture and design. His first success came in 1894, when his plan was chosen in a competition to design a new building for the Art School – an achievement for which he did not receive public credit, either from his firm or the press. In the next few years he took commissions for a variety of work, the most notable complete and extant examples of which are the School of Art, Queen's Cross Church and Scotland St School in Glasgow; Windyhill in Kilmacolm; and The Hill House in Helensburgh, which is now owned by the National Trust for Scotland. His greatest patron was the tearoom owner, Kate **Cranston**.

His style Mackintosh was the first Scottish architect since Robert **Adam** in the 18th century to concern himself with interiors. He conceived total schemes of design, including the building and everything in it, from furniture and textiles to metalwork, wall decoration and lighting. His architecture was strikingly modern, with strong recti-linear composition, but it did not ignore its histor-ical environment – it was based on tradition-al Scottish vernacular, and echoes of the style are evident in his building.

Continental acclaim Mackintosh's work was noticed by the Viennese Secessionists who invited him to design the interior of a flat for the Vienna Exhibition of 1900. His contribution caused a sensation. (While he was in Vienna Mackintosh was asked to design a room for a music lover; his final plans for this appeared in a set of drawings, *Haus Eines Kunstfreundes, The House of an Art Lover*, which were published in 1902. The Art Lover's House has recently been built in Glasgow's Bellahouston Park, and is due to be opened in 1995.) Mackintosh's reputation on the Continent was made overnight. At the Turin exhibition in 1902, the Scottish pavilion was designed almost entirely by him. He exhibited in Venice, Munich, Dresden, Budapest and Moscow, and every one of his exhibits was eagerly bought up.

Difficulties at home Mackintosh was now at the peak of his fame: an architect of European standing, he was the leading exponent of Art Nouveau and the major figure of its Scottish expression, the Glasgow Style. But, ironically, his work was not valued at home, and commissions dried up. Mackintosh's architecture was more tempered to art than to commercial practice and he was temperamentally unsuited to the constraints imposed by office routine. He alienated his fellow-partners, and eventually resigned in 1913.

Marriage to Margaret Macdonald Mackintosh's collaborator in much of his interior design was his wife, Margaret Macdonald, one of the group known as the **Glasgow Girls**; she had a considerable influence on the development of his style. He and Margaret had met at the Art School and married in 1900. Although she herself was a gifted artist, Margaret's time and energy was largely given to nurturing and emotionally sustaining her husband's talent, which she believed was of true genius. The couple were deeply in love and their marriage was a happy one. They had no children, possibly because Margaret did not wish any.

Exile and watercolour work Unrecognised as a genius in his own land, Mackintosh left Glasgow in 1914, moving first to London and later to France. He confined his work to his studio, concentrating on watercolours, and further emphasised his innate talents by emerging as one of the finest British exponents of the medium.

Standing The sense of lost opportunity in surveying Mackintosh's career is overwhelming. He was always aware of his own genius and felt deeply his failure to be recognised. He died of cancer in London in 1928, almost forgotten. Today his work fetches huge sums at auction and is exhibited in museums of modern art around the world. He is seen as a prophet of the Modern Movement and as a founder of modern architecture. His talent has at last been recognised in his home country, and, ironically, he stands as one of the most famous of Scots.

Alistair Maclean
1922–1987
Writer

Early life Alistair Maclean was born in Glasgow and brought up in the Highlands, returning to the city after the Second World War to attend the university. During the war he served in the Royal Navy, and the adventures and experiences he had during that time stood him in good stead as material for some of his most successful novels.

Competition success Maclean trained as a schoolteacher and took up writing in a bid to supplement his income. In 1954 he entered a short-story-writing competition in the *Glasgow Herald*, winning first prize with an action-packed naval adventure story. He was commissioned by Collins, the Glasgow publishers, to produce a novel in a similar vein, and *HMS Ulysses* appeared the following year. The book was an instant popular success, and a similar reception for *The Guns of Navarone* in 1956 encouraged him to give up teaching to write full time.

His work Maclean's stock-in-trade was the adventure thriller, often with a naval or other service background. The geographical settings for his books were wide-ranging, from Florida for *Fear is the Key* in 1961, to the Antarctic in *Ice Station Zebra* in 1963 and Scotland for *When Eight Bells Toll* three years after that. His literary output was large, but not confined to one genre; other work included biographies of Captain Cook and T. E. Lawrence, as well as a Western novel (*Breakheart Pass*). He sold over 200 million books throughout the world, and many of his titles were made into successful films.

Later life Maclean moved to Switzerland after he became established and, apart from a short period spent as a hotel owner in Cornwall in the mid 1960s, lived there for the rest of his life. He died of an alcohol-related illness in 1987.

John Maclean
1879–1923
Marxist politician

Highland background John Maclean was born in Glasgow into a family of Highland origin who had been cleared off their land. His father died when he was nine and his mother took several jobs to ensure her children were educated. John went to teacher training college and later took his degree at Glasgow University.

War and revolution Maclean's socialism was of a revolutionary kind, and he was already regarded with suspicion by the authorities by the time war broke out in 1914. He was convinced of the efficacy of education in the process of politicisation, and after he was sacked from his local education authority teaching post in 1915 he became a full-time Marxist lecturer and organiser, holding open classes which regularly attracted over a thousand people. One of his students was James **Maxton**. Maclean later founded the Scottish Labour College. He also spoke against conscription and the war, moving from calling for a negotiated settlement to demanding revolution. He was arrested and imprisoned in 1916, but the February revolution in Russia the next year led to left-wing demonstrations in Glasgow, and Maclean was released. He emerged with his ideas reinforced, preaching revolution. His efforts were recognised by the government in Moscow, who made him Soviet Consul in Scotland. He was imprisoned again in 1918, being released only after the armistice.

Isolation Maclean's final years were spent trying to organise a Scottish Communist Party and working against counter-revolution in Russia. He was increasingly isolated from his friends among the 'Red Clydesiders', who favoured democratic means of achieving their aims and who found his uncompromising purist views too extreme. Arrested six times, his health was broken by his treatment and force feeding in jail, and he died in 1923.

George MacLeod
1895–1991
Founder of the Iona Community

War service and the ministry George Fielden MacLeod was the second son of a Glasgow MP and was born in the city in 1895. He was educated at Oxford University and went on to see distinguished service during the First World War, when he was awarded the MC and the Croix de Guerre. He returned to Scotland after the war to study theology at Edinburgh, and was minister in the city from 1926 to 1930, when he made a name for himself as a superb preacher. He moved to Govan in Glasgow in 1930.

Controversial public life He was one of the most prominent churchmen of his day and in 1957–58 became moderator of the General Assembly, the Church of Scotland's governing body. While in office he created controversy by supporting a plan to reconcile the Churches of Scotland and England which would have seen the reintroduction of a form of episcopacy to the Scottish church. The scheme was eventually dropped. MacLeod was also an outspoken socialist and a writer and broadcaster, and in 1986 he saw one of his cherished aims realised when the General Assembly voted against the use of nuclear weapons by the British Government under any circumstances.

Iona Community MacLeod's primary fame comes from two sources, each achieved in the teeth of bitter opposition from suspicious members of the Church establishment. Firstly, he was the leader of the dedicated group established in the 1930s to restore **Columba**'s monastery on the holy island of Iona; and secondly, inseparable from the restoration, he was the founder of the Iona Community, reviving in a 20th-century context the missionary spirit of Iona's first settlers in deprived city areas.

George MacLeod succeeded to his father's baronetcy in 1924. He never used the title but he did accept a life peerage in 1967.

J. J. R. Macleod
1876–1935
Co-discoverer of insulin

Early career success John James Rickard Macleod was a physiologist and teacher who devoted most of his working life to the investigation and treatment of diabetes. He was the son of a minister, born at New Clunie near Dunkeld. He graduated in medicine from Aberdeen University in 1898 and spent the next few years working on the Continent and in London. In 1902 he became lecturer in biochemistry at the London Hospital, and the following year, although only 27 years old, was appointed professor of physiology at the Western Reserve University in Cleveland, Ohio.

Discovery of insulin It was from this time that Macleod's interest in diabetes dated; between 1905 and 1921 he published 37 papers on related topics. It was known that a malfunction in the pancreas prevented the build-up of sugar levels in the bloodstream, but the cause had still not been identified by 1920 when Macleod, now at the University of Toronto, was approached by Dr Frederick Banting for help in conducting his researches. Working to Banting's theories with Macleod's facilities, guidance and advice, the assembled team identified the pancreatic malfunction and isolated the hormone which controlled blood sugar levels. Macleod gave the hormone the name 'insulin'. In 1923 Macleod and Banting were awarded the Nobel Prize for Medicine, which they shared with their fellow researchers.

Later work Although primarily interested in diabetes, Macleod researched other areas, including air sickness, electric shock and the TB bacterium. He was also committed to medical education and was an outstanding teacher. In 1928 he was appointed regius professor of physiology at Aberdeen, a post he held, despite disability in his later years, until his death in 1935.

James Macpherson
1736–1796
Poet

Early life The most famous of Scottish writers in his day, James Macpherson's name is now almost forgotten. A farmer's son, he was born at Ruthven and educated at King's College, Aberdeen. He went to Edinburgh to study divinity, but returned north to become a teacher.

Fingal and *Temora* In 1736 Macpherson published his first work, an epic poem called *The Highlander*. He subsequently fell in with members of the Edinburgh literary establishment who encouraged him to publish fragments of ancient poetry he had. These appeared in 1760 to a remarkable reception. Macpherson claimed that these were only fragments of a 9,000-line epic Gaelic poem by Ossian, warrior poet and son of the legendary hero, Fingal. He was sent off by patrons on a tour of the Highlands and islands to find the remainder of the poem and publish it in translation. The result, *Fingal*, which appeared in 1761, caused a sensation and was rapturously received across Europe: Byron and Goethe admired it, and Napoleon, who was enthralled, never travelled without a copy. However, it was not long before debate raged over its authenticity, fired by Dr Johnson among others. In fact, the poem was a mixture of bits of verse, ballads and oral history, with Macpherson's own work to bulk it up. It was followed by a second epic poem, *Temora*, in 1763. Macpherson never produced evidence to show the 'translations' were substantially anything other than his own work.

Later wealth In 1763 he forsook poetry to become surveyor general of the Floridas, and in later life in London became very wealthy through his mercantile interests. He died on the estate he bought for himself at Badenoch, and was buried at his own expense in Westminster Abbey.

St Margaret
c. 1046–1093
Saint and Queen of Scots

Margaret, canonised by Pope Innocent IV in 1251 a century and a half after her death, is the only Scottish royal saint.

Flight into Scotland Margaret was actually a member of the ancient English royal family and was a descendent of King Alfred. Her father, Edward, the son of King Edmund Ironside, gained the name 'the Exile' because of his European stay during the reign in England of the Danish King Canute. Margaret herself was born during his exile, probably in Hungary. Her young brother, Edgar the Aetheling, had a very strong claim to the throne after the death of King Harold during the Conquest of 1066, but he instead came to terms with the Duke of Normandy, William the Conqueror. But the suspicions of the Normans meant that the family's position was always precarious, and they finally fled north from Northumbria. It is probable that they were headed for the Continent again, but their ship was blown off course and they came ashore at Fife.

Royal suitor Such an important family were naturally given a royal reception. The King of Scots, Malcolm III, known as Malcolm Canmore (or Great Head), had been married, but his wife died in 1068. He set his sights on Margaret as his queen but she refused his proposals, preferring, according to one account, a life of piety as a virgin. However, Malcolm was the family's protector, and to refuse his repeated requests would have put them in a difficult situation. Consequently, Malcolm and Margaret were finally married at Dunfermline in 1069. It is certain that Malcolm deeply loved his wife. He set great store by her opinions, and frequently went to great lengths to please her. Despite being unable to read or write himself, he once bought her a religious text which he then had set in gold and adorned with precious jewels.

Her influence and piety Margaret brought a degree of refinement to the Scottish court, as well as a great deal of personal wealth. She anglicised the court, too, bringing in English customs and language in place of Gaelic, which she never learned to speak. Her influence with her husband also meant that she was allowed a hand in setting the agenda for the Church in Scotland. She brought in a European uniformity of religious practice, in the process making inroads into the sway of the Celtic Church in the north of the country. Margaret was personally pious, too: she cared for orphans, whom she often fed from her own spoon; she washed the feet of the poor; she ransomed the English captives of her husband's Northumbrian raids; and she damaged her own health through prolonged fasting and abstinence. Her piety was also passed on to her children, three whom – Edgar, Alexander and David – became kings of Scots.

Her death Margaret was ill for over a year before her death, and as she lay on her deathbed news of the death in battle of Malcolm and of Edward, her eldest son, was brought to her by Edgar. Her last words were to thank God for the pain brought by their deaths which might cleanse the sin from her own soul. She died four days later and was buried in Dunfermline Abbey.

Mary
1542–1587
Queen of Scots

Enduring appeal Mary, Queen of Scots is the most romantic figure in Scottish history. Variously seen as impulsive and led astray by her sexual passions, as a Catholic martyr, or as a lively and attractive young woman overcome by dour, hypocritical, middle-aged men, she has sustained as much interest in the centuries since her death as she attracted during her life.

Childhood Mary became queen after the death of her father, **James V**, when she was only six days old. Henry VIII of England soon decided that she would make a suitable bride for his son, Edward, but the Scots concluded a treaty with France, and in 1548 Mary was sent away for her own safety, as prospective bride of the Dauphin Francis, the future king.

Queen of France Mary was brought up and educated at the French court with the royal children, and all her early influences were French. (It was from her practice that the spelling of the royal house's name changed to the Frenchified 'Stuart'.) She and the sickly Francis were married in 1558, and the couple became king and queen on the death of his father in 1559. But by the end of 1560 Francis was dead and the power of the house of Guise, Mary's family, eclipsed at court. She left France for Scotland in August 1561 and landed at Leith on a foggy east-coast morning.

Inhospitable Scots Her mother, the regent, had died in 1560 with the country in the throes of Reformation upheavals and on the brink of all-out civil war, so the task which faced the 18-year-old Catholic queen was immense. The difficulties of her new life were brought sharply home when she attended Mass in her private chapel on her first Sunday; a riot and threats to kill the priest were thwarted only by the personal intervention of her illegitimate half-brother Lord James Stewart. He was head of the Protestant

party and one of the most powerful men in the country, and Mary advanced him in 1562 to the title of Earl of Moray. As her adviser, he helped her steer a course through the stormy political and religious waters. Her charm and personal fearlessness also endeared her to many of her nobles, with whom she hunted. In the evenings she read Latin with George **Buchanan**, who was friendly at this time. But not all Protestant subjects were so accommodating. Both her gender and her religion were an affront to John **Knox**, one of the Reformation leaders, and he decried her at every opportunity. He complained on the one hand that she was 'very grave' in council, and on the other that in the company of friends and musicians, 'then might be seen skipping not very comely for honest women'. Mary, in turn, invited him into her presence to debate with her and, despite his biased record of events, his hints that she had a 'crafty wit' suggest that she bested him on several occasions.

Marriage to Darnley Mary always believed the English throne, then held by her Protestant cousin, Elizabeth, to be hers by right, and the hope of gaining it was one of the main reasons for her marriage in July 1565. Her new husband, Henry Stewart, Lord **Darnley** (right), was her cousin, and he also had a strong claim. Mary also hoped his strength would help her break free of her advisers, including her powerful half-brother, and let her follow her own policies. She was also in love with her husband, calling him 'the best proportionit lang man that sche had ever seen'. But Darnley, vain, weak and ambitious beyond his talents, was a political and personal disaster. His jealous participation in the murder of Mary's Italian

secretary, David Rizzio, in the pregnant queen's presence only months after their marriage, was an unforgivable betrayal. Mary affected a reconciliation with him at the birth of their son, the future **James VI**, in June 1566, but by the christening in December the estrangement was again evident when Darnley stayed sulking in his room. There was talk of divorce, but Mary was anxious that her son's legitimacy should not be questioned.

Marriage to Bothwell Mary was now isolated from her husband and her advisers, leaving the Earl of **Bothwell** as her only loyal ally. He was almost certainly a party to the murder of Darnley at Kirk o' Field, outside Edinburgh, in February 1567, although he was cleared at a trial two months later. Mary's guilt was also suspected but nothing was ever proved. At the end of April he boldly abducted the queen, apparently raping her before marrying her in May 1567.

Fall and escape to England Her second improvident Scottish marriage sealed Mary's fate by uniting all her opponents. Mary and

Bothwell's forces were defeated at Carberry Hill in June when the queen was brought back to Edinburgh to face public humiliation before the city mob, and imprisonment in Lochleven Castle. There her reign officially ended when, under threat of death, she abdicated the throne in favour of her infant son. She escaped 11 months later only to face her final military defeat at Langside on 13 May. Three days later, in fear of her life, Mary crossed the border into England.

Trial A commission of inquiry was set up in England to examine the recent affairs in Scotland. Technically, it could have led to Mary's restoration but for the fact that it was rigged from the outset. The queen was not allowed to attend, and the so-called Casket Letters, purportedly written by Mary to Bothwell, were produced as evidence of their plot against Darnley. The original letters have disappeared but it is assumed that they were letters written to Bothwell by someone else, but tampered with and forged in an effort to blacken the queen's name.

Intrigue and execution Mary remained in custody, yet negotiations continued between her agents and the ultra-cautious Elizabeth of England to achieve a solution whereby Mary could rule jointly with her son. These were hampered by a succession of plots to free Mary and place her on the English throne. Finally in 1586 English officials trapped her into agreeing to the Babington plot to assassinate Elizabeth. Her fate was sealed: her trial at Fotheringhay Castle in October had a pre-ordained outcome, and Elizabeth, although unwilling to take the responsibility, signed her cousin's death warrant on 1 February 1587. Mary was executed, showing great courage and dignity, seven days later.

James Maxton
1885–1946
Labour politician

Changing political allegiances   James Maxton was born at
Pollokshaws in Glasgow into a teaching family: both his parents
were teachers, he and his three sisters all later became teachers,
and he was to marry a teacher. His political affiliations in his early
years were Conservative, but after hearing a speech by the Labour
politician Philip Snowden in 1904 he joined the ILP. He graduated from Glasgow University in 1909.

Conviction politics   Maxton faced difficulties during the First
World War for his anti-war stance. He spent a year in prison, and
his dog was stoned to death by some of his opponents. In the
1918 General Election he stood as a candidate in Bridgeton in
Glasgow's east end, and although he was unsuccessful he later persuaded the victor to join the ILP. In 1922 he finally won the seat,
which he held until his death. He quickly made his presence felt
in Parliament, and was expelled from the Commons in 1923 during a debate on reducing health expenditure, when he called some
of his fellow MPs 'murderers'. He was also bitterly opposed to the
leadership of Ramsay **MacDonald**, and led the split of the ILP
from the Labour Party in 1932. The move left him relatively isolated from the mainstream of labour politics.

Personal life   Maxton was devastated by his wife's death in 1922
but found happiness in a second marriage in 1935. His health was
poor in later years and he died in 1946 after a long illness.

His appeal   Much of Maxton's fame rests on his oratorical skills
and his immense personal charm. Although a conviction politician, a student of John **Maclean** and one of the foremost of the
fiery 'Red Clydesiders', he never used dry, formulaic dogma, preferring to entertain and persuade his audiences with wit and
humour. He was among the best-loved contemporary politicians.

James Clerk Maxwell
1831–1879
Physicist

Early genius   James Clerk Maxwell was the son of John Clerk, an Edinburgh lawyer who later adopted the additional surname of Maxwell to take possession of an estate left to the family in Kirkcudbrightshire. James was born in Edinburgh and later attended the university there. His brilliance was evident at an early age; when he was 15 he had a paper published by the Royal Society of Edinburgh. Maxwell went on to study at Cambridge, and at the age of only 25 was appointed professor of natural philosophy at Marischal College. He later worked in London before moving back to his Kirkcudbrightshire estate after the death of his father in 1865 to concentrate on his researches. However, he was tempted south once more when offered the new post of professor of experimental physics at Cambridge in 1871.

Discoveries and advances   Maxwell was a theorist but the practical applications of his revolutionary work surround our lives in the modern world. His most important work, published in 1873 in *Treatise on Electricity and Magnetism*, examined the nature of electromagnetism and laid the way for the work of Einstein and Planck. As well as discoveries in this field, he completed a range of other research from the nature of Saturn's rings, whose composition he proved mathematically, and the kinetic theory of gases, to the perception of colour and a demonstration of colour photography, using as his subject a piece of tartan ribbon.

Character   Despite the awe-inspiring nature of his work and theories, Maxwell always remained a deeply religious man. A creative and mathematical genius, he was also a patient and kind teacher, with a sense of humour and fun. Although he died at the early age of 48, his immense intellect and the work he completed rank him on a par with Newton and Einstein.

Andrew Melville
1545–1622
Religious and academic reformer

After John **Knox**, Andrew Melville is the most famous figure of the Scottish Reformation.

University reforms He studied at St Andrews, Paris, Poitiers and Geneva, the foremost centre of reformed religious thought at the time. Melville's experience of Continental universities coupled with his strength of personality made him an ideal reformer of the Scottish university system. He spent six years as principal at Glasgow from 1574 before being appointed to St Andrews. He brought the ailing and old-fashioned Scottish universities into line with teaching methods and practices in Europe.

Church v King However, Melville is best remembered for his contribution to the fervent religious and political debates of the time. Religious reform had come relatively late to Scotland; by 1560 most modern thought followed the example of Geneva with its presbyterian system of church government. Melville was a fervent presbyterian, favouring the exclusion of lay (or royal) authority from the Church. This brought him into conflict with **James VI**: in his most famous outbursts, Melville told James that he was merely 'God's silly vassal', and 'not a king, nor a lord, nor a head, but a member' of the kingdom of Christ in Scotland. Melville, supported by an eager Church, was a thorn in James' side for years, albeit one which became easier to bear at 400 miles' remove after the king's accession to the English throne in 1603. James summoned Melville to London in 1606 and subsequently threw him in the Tower. He was not released until 1611, when he left Britain to teach theology at Sedan.

The outcome James won the battle, successfully imposing episcopacy on the Church, but the presbyterians ultimately won the war, and their system of church government endures today.

Hugh Miller
1802–1856
Geologist

Science v religion Hugh Miller personified the tensions between the new science of geology, which he single-handedly popularised, and the old certainties of religion. But they were tensions he could not reconcile, and he shot himself at Christmas in 1856.

Melancholy personality Hugh Miller was born at Cromarty. His father, a sailor, drowned in the Moray Firth when Hugh was five years old, and his mother became a seamstress to bring in money for the family. She was descended from a Gaelic seer, and may have developed a fey and melancholy turn of mind in her son: he had a dark and obsessive side to his personality, and all his life believed in fairies, bogles and ghosts, and was subject to hallucinations.

Early career and marriage When he was 16 he was apprenticed as stonemason, working with his uncle in local quarries. His profession intensified his interest in rocks and the fossils in them, but he had to give up the work after contracting silicosis from the stone dust. He later became a monumental mason, and it was while carving a tombstone in 1831 that he met Lydia Falconer, who became his wife. An intelligent, refined woman, she came from a well-to-do family who opposed her attachment to a man of lower social standing. The pair were considering emigration to America when in 1834 Miller was offered a post as bank accountant in Inverness, a position more acceptable to Lydia's parents and which would allow him to support a family.

Theology and geology Miller continued his geological researches and also found time to write and publish a selection of poems and folk tales. But his career took another turn in 1839 when he came to the notice of Thomas **Chalmers**' evangelical party in the Church of Scotland. Miller was invited to edit the movement's paper, *The Witness*. He was an immediate success, and circulation soared. Miller used the paper as a platform to publish his geological findings; as a self-educated man, he could avoid the use of scientific jargon, and was able to articulate difficult concepts in geology and theology simply and humorously. He supported the establishment of the Free Church in 1843, but many in the Church were uneasy at his idiosyncratic ideas, and he gradually became distanced from them.

Problems of his conclusions By the mid 19th century it was recognised that fossils were simpler than their modern-day descendants, suggesting the possibility of development of species and calling into question their fixed nature. For Miller, such a progression compromised the spiritual essence of humanity, and was unacceptable. Yet he never took refuge in any safe fundamentalist haven, being driven to pursue his researches and confront honestly the conclusions to which they led him. In his later years he was increasingly in darkness, preoccupied with fear of the supernatural, the problems in the Church and reconciling geology and religion. Finally, after correcting the proofs of his *Testimony of the Rocks* on 23 December, his mind bent under the strain, and he killed himself. Darwin's *Origin of Species* was published three years after Miller's death, and the problems which he had confronted so bravely are still being debated today.

Lord Monboddo
1714–1799
Judge and eccentric

James Burnett was born at Monboddo in Kincardineshire. He became an advocate in 1737 and Lord of Session in 1767, taking the judicial title, 'Lord Monboddo'.

Proto-anthropologist Although a competent judge Monboddo preferred the pursuit of his private interests to the law; these were mainly the study of anthropology and society. He disputed the Biblical version of the origin of language as divine judgement for the Tower of Babel, asserting that language developed naturally. He also emphasised a relationship between humans and monkeys, claiming that the orang-utang's lack of speech was merely an accident. Some of these views seem to anticipate Darwin, but at the time they were greeted with ridicule by his opponents and embarrassment by his friends.

Eccentricities Monboddo was thought eccentric in his habits. He venerated Greek learning and philosophy, and tried to copy the simplicity of the lives of the ancients. Until he was well into his 80s he made annual trips to London on horseback, refusing to travel by carriage (not the way in the ancient world) because he considered the practice effeminate. In summer he retired to his estate to live a simple life. His lands did not bring in much money, but he never raised rents or evicted tenants.

Personal life Monboddo was a kind-hearted man who delighted in the society of friends, numbering among them some of the most distinguished men in society, including **Black**, **Hume** and **Smith**. But his life was crossed by sorrow: his wife died in childbirth; his only son died young; and his younger daughter, whose beauty was celebrated in **Burns**' *Address to Edinburgh*, died of TB at 25. Monboddo himself died of a stroke, succeeded only by his elder daughter, who married an eminent Greek scholar.

Marquess of Montrose
1612–1650
Royalist soldier and poet

Reputation The fifth Earl and first Marquess of Montrose, James Graham is undoubtedly one of the most dashing and glamorous figures to cross the pages of Scottish history. His personality was such that his reputation was only enhanced, rather than destroyed by his execution in 1650.

Youth Born at Montrose, the young James was educated at St Andrews University, and in 1626 he succeeded to his father's title of Earl of Montrose. In 1629, while he was still an undergraduate and only 17, he was married to Madeleine, one of the six beautiful daughters of Lord Carnegie. The couple stayed with her father until Montrose's coming of age at 21, when he set off for a three-year tour on the Continent.

Covenanter The Scotland to which Montrose returned was in a religious ferment over the liturgical changes which Charles I was introducing into the Church of Scotland. In 1638 Montrose was one of the many prominent Church members who signed the National Covenant in protest at the innovations. Although he became Charles' champion in the battles that followed, Montrose never wavered from the support he had given the aims of the National Covenant. He conducted a campaign in the north-east on behalf of the Covenanters, but became increasingly alienated by extremists within the movement and by those, such as the Earl of Argyll, whom he perceived merely to be using the civil and religious turmoil to further their own political interests. By 1640 he had joined the king's camp. Despite this apparent switching of sides, Montrose was one of the few in the Scotland of the 1630s and '40s whose position and principles remained constant.

Royalist The early 1640s saw the Scots' religious grievances pull them into the Civil War in England, and in 1644 a Covenanter force was despatched to fight for the English Parliament against the king. Montrose had spent several months imprisoned by the Covenanters in Edinburgh Castle, but after his release Charles created him marquess and his lieutenant-general in Scotland. On 18 August 1644 Montrose came north, crossing the border disguised as a groom, with only two followers. Within two weeks he had met up with a Scottish–Irish force led by Alistair Macdonald, rallied others and defeated a Covenanter army at Tippermuir.

Brilliant campaign In the next 12 months Montrose won a series of five more pitched battles against the Covenanter forces in a tactically brilliant and breathtakingly daring campaign which took him at great speed from one side of Scotland to the other and back again. His arch-enemy, Argyll, was ignominiously chased before him on at least three occasions and once had to flee his own castle while Montrose's men laid waste his lands. However, after his most notable victory, at Kilsyth, almost a year to the day after his return, many of his Highland troops went home, leaving him with a much-depleted force. The following month at Philiphaugh Montrose's troops were surprised by a Covenanter army newly arrived from England. Montrose himself just managed to escape, and returned to the Highlands. After trying in vain to raise more troops, he set sail for Norway in 1646.

Exile and betrayal Montrose spent the next few years on the Continent, being well received wherever he went. He was constantly in touch with the situation at home, however; when news of the king's execution reached him in 1649 he was so overcome that he fainted. He swore to avenge Charles' death, and in 1650 set sail again for Scotland. But his luck had deserted him: he lost much of his little army in a shipwreck off Orkney; his forces were heavily defeated in battle at Carbisdale; he was forced to hide as a fugitive in the Highlands, and almost starved to death; and, finally, he was betrayed for £25,000 by Macleod of Assynt, from whom he had sought shelter.

His panache Montrose's reputation rests not only on his skill as a tactician and soldier, but on his personal conduct, especially in the last weeks of his life. He was brought to Edinburgh, where he had already been tried and sentenced to death in his absence. He faced his accusers in Parliament with great dignity. The execution was to be carried out on 21 May, and Montrose dressed for the event with panache, wearing a bright scarlet cassock and appearing, as one observer said, more like a bridegroom than a criminal. When mocked by one of his enemies for the care with which he dressed his hair, he replied, 'My head is still my own; tonight, when it will be yours, treat it as you please.' His body was cut down from the gallows and quartered, his limbs being sent to the four principal cities in the kingdom.

Epitaph Montrose was not only a soldier, he was also a talented poet and Scotland's only composer of Cavalier courtly poetry. His *My Dear and Only Love* demonstrates his loyalty to the king and the nobility of his ideals, while perhaps his finest epitaph also is contained in his own lines, from *To His Mistress*: 'He either fears his fate too much / Or his Deserts are small, / That puts it not unto the Touch / To win or lose it all.'

John Muir
1838–1914
American ecologist and conservationist

Early American experiences John Muir was born in Dunbar but emigrated with his family at the age of 11 to Wisconsin in the American Mid-West. The interest in the natural world which came easy to the Scots boy was deepened, despite the need to work hard on his father's farm. His relationship with his father, a domineering Calvinist, was never easy; John had to rise each night at 1 a.m. to read in secret the books he was forbidden by his tyrannical and puritanical father. His midnight work paid off, and he was accepted by the University of Wisconsin to study, among other subjects, biology. His studies were interrupted by the Civil War (1861–65), when his anti-war beliefs took him to Canada to escape being drafted. Here he first learned to survive on his own in the wilderness, while keeping notes of his botanical observations in his journals.

Yosemite Valley After the war Muir decided to explore systematically the American wilderness. Alone and on foot, he travelled through forests, mountains, valleys and meadows, filling books with sketches and descriptions of the plants, animals and trees he loved. In 1868 he first encountered California's Yosemite Valley, one of the most spectacular areas on earth and the place which was to occupy a major place in his life and work.

Birth of American conservationism By the mid 1870s he was convinced that the frontier was at an end, and that even though national resources then seemed inexhaustible, the freedom to destroy irreplaceable forests had to be curtailed. His public crusading for the retention of the wilderness made him a centre around which the young conservation movement grew.

National Parks Muir married in 1880, and he and his wife had two daughters. He dropped out of public view for several years, working on father-in-law's fruit farm in California. During this time he developed his ideas, and his return to public life, with his wife's encouragement, saw him spearhead the drive to have established a national park at Yosemite, based on conservation principles. Muir developed the ideas and is now recognised as the founder of the national parks movement. He saw his dream realised in 1890. To emphasise the new conservation movement's principles and to educate the park's visitors in conservation, Muir founded the Sierra Club in 1892, and served as its first president.

Isolation and decline But at the start of the new century Muir was isolated: he was seen as too extreme in his desire to preserve the wilderness untarnished; his wife died in 1905; and he was engaged in a hard battle against a plan to flood part of Yosemite National Park to create a reservoir to supply San Francisco's water. Worn out by the struggle and broken-hearted at his failure, he died in 1914.

Mysticism Muir's views were not simply based on ideas, but sprang from a holistic view of creation and a feeling of oneness with the natural world. He was a mystic who often slept out under the stars and once climbed a tree to share its experiences during a storm. He famously declared, 'When we try to pick out anything by itself, we find it hitched to everything else in the universe'.

Legacy Although relatively unknown in his native country, Muir is famous and popular in the US, where his books have rarely been out of print. He is recognised as the first discoverer and publiciser of the American wilderness and the founder of the modern conservation movement.

St Mungo
c. 520–612
Patron saint of Glasgow

Birth and childhood Mungo's mother was St Thenew, Christian daughter of a pagan king of Lothian. Her father ordered her execution after she was raped and became pregnant, and she was cast out onto the Firth of Forth in a coracle. Her boat was washed ashore at Culross, where she gave birth to a son. She and her baby were looked after by St Serf in his monastery there, and he baptised them both. The child's name was Kentigern, but his nickname was Mungo, which means 'dear friend'. Under his mother's and Serf's guidance, Mungo became a missionary.

Missionary work He built on the Christian legacy left in southern Scotland by the Romans, and travelled to the neighbouring kingdom of Strathclyde, preaching, establishing a monastery and building a little wooden church at Glasgow. In 543 he was made Bishop of Cumbria, then including parts of southern Scotland. His missionary work was not confined to Scotland; after 553 when civil war broke out in Strathclyde he spent several years in Wales, where he is said to have met St David. In 584, back in Scotland, he was visited by **Columba**. He is buried in St Mungo's Cathedral in Glasgow, although his original church was replaced by a stone-built one in medieval times.

Glasgow As the city's patron saint, Mungo appears on Glasgow's coat of arms along with pictorial mementoes of his miracles: a frozen branch he made burn in the dead of winter; a bird for St Serf's pet robin Mungo brought back to life; a bell he was sent by the pope; and a fish with a ring in its mouth, for the lost ring of the queen of Strathclyde which her suspicious husband demanded she wear. Mungo told her the ring would be found in the mouth of the first salmon pulled from the Clyde, thus saving the queen from death at the hands of her jealous spouse.

Lord George Murray
c. 1700–1760
Jacobite commander

Talents 'Had Prince **Charles** slept during the whole of the expedition, and allowed Lord George Murray to act for him according to his own judgement, he would have found the crown of Great Britain on his head when he awoke.' This was the judgement of one of his fellows on the foremost Jacobite general.

Military training Lord George Murray was the fifth son of the 1st Duke of Atholl. Like many younger sons of the landed classes, he spent much of his youth serving in Continental armies, although he was committed enough to the Jacobite cause to be present at the risings of 1715 and 1719.

Successes in 1745–46 Murray joined the Forty-five only after persuasion from his brother, but his military skills were such that Charles immediately appointed him lieutenant-general. He was a fearless soldier and leader and a brilliant tactician, winning spectacular victories at Prestonpans and Falkirk, as well as conducting the steady Jacobite advance as far south as Derby and, perhaps most impressively, the safe retreat back to Scotland.

Disagreement, defeat and exile Murray and the prince disagreed over the retreat and subsequent tactics; Murray was particularly against Charles' march north to Inverness, and his decision to fight at Culloden. Despite this, he fought on the right wing, resigning his post only the day after. The Duke of Cumberland, leader of the Hanoverian forces, tried to blacken Murray's name with documents suggesting he had ordered that no quarter be given to prisoners; they were shown to be forgeries and attempts by Cumberland to excuse his own savagery in the Highlands. Murray went into exile and was well received, with accommodation and a pension, by the prince's father in Rome, but his breach with Charles was never fully healed. He died in Holland.

Lady Nairne
1766–1845
Songwriter

Jacobite background Carolina Oliphant was born at Gask in Perthshire into a strongly Jacobite family who had fought in both the risings of 1715 and 1745. Named after Prince **Charles** Edward Stuart, Carolina was known as the 'Flower of Strathearn' because of her youthful beauty. In 1806 she married her second cousin, William, Major Nairne, who later succeeded to his family's title of 'Lord Nairne'.

Songs In the early 1790s Carolina became interested in **Burns'** reworking of old Scots songs. She, too, began collecting traditional airs, to which she wrote her own words. With her family background and influences, it was not surprising that the Jacobite cause became the subject of much of her work, including her best songs. She wrote the stirring *The Hundred Pipers*, *Charlie is my Darlin'*, and the haunting lament for the lost cause, *Will ye no' come back again?* However, she kept her work a secret even from her husband, and it was not until the early 1820s that it began to appear under a pseudonym. As well as Jacobite songs she wrote airs such as *The Rowan Tree* and *The Auld Hoose*.

After her husband's death in 1830, Lady Nairne travelled throughout Europe, finally returning to Gask two years before her death to live with her nephew and his wife in the new house which had been built there, the 'auld' one of her song having been demolished. Before her death she gave permission for her collected songs, 87 in all, to be published. They appeared as *Lays from Strathearn*, and were ultimately published posthumously.

Appeal of her work Lady Nairne's songs are simple and direct in their appeal to the emotions. Her Jacobite songs are her best known and best loved of her work, and she stands second only to Burns as author of the most popular Scottish songs.

John Napier
1550–1617
Discoverer of logarithms

John Napier was born at Merchiston. He was educated at St Andrews then travelled on the Continent until 1571.

Diversions He was always interested in the sciences, but in the turbulent period of the Reformation such a devout Calvinist as Napier was easily diverted into theological study and writing. He enthusiastically pursued religious controversy and his fear of a Spanish Catholic invasion led to the dissipation of his creative talents in devising machines of war, including primitive tanks.

Persistent character Napier was a man of great intellect, persistence and will, making him well fitted for his life's work of solitary study. It also meant he was a vigorous opponent in the many disputes he had with his father, relatives, neighbours and with Edinburgh town council for their building of a house for plague victims on his lands. Other diverse pursuits included a search for hidden treasure at a neighbour's castle and experiments with fertilisers. His solitary lifestyle and interests in subjects like divination acquired him a reputation as a necromancer.

Logarithms But in the 1590s Napier was concentrating on his mathematical researches. He had grasped the underlying principle of logarithms – a name he devised – and his later years were spent developing his theories, computing the logarithms and constructing tables. In the course of his researches he was also the first to devise the use of the decimal point. In 1614 his first book, *Descriptio*, described the tables and their application in trigonometry and numerology. He also invented the world's first mechanical computing device in the form of a series of rods which were nicknamed 'Napier's Bones'. *Constructio*, published after his death, described how he constructed the log tables, but he never disclosed the means by which he made his discoveries.

St Ninian
Lived c. 400
Missionary and saint

First missionary   Relatively little is known about St Ninian, but he was certainly the earliest missionary sent out to Scotland from Rome to convert the people to Christianity. According to one chronicle Ninian was of Welsh origin, but another claimed he was the son of a recently converted Christian king and was born in the south west. He received his training in Rome and was sent back by the pope as a bishop with instruction to convert the inhabitants of west Britain. On his way home Ninian is said to have stopped to visit Martin of Tours and asked him for stonemasons to help him build his church.

Establishing in Britain   By this time Christianity was the religion of the Roman Empire, so it was natural that Ninian should base himself in an area not far from Carlisle, the biggest centre in the north of Roman Britain. Whithorn was his chosen spot for his church, Candida Casa, dedicated to St Martin of Tours. He also built a monastery for the training of more missionaries.

Success and difficulties   Ninian's mission was relatively successful, building on some of the networks the Romans had left and going on to bring in new converts in not only the south west, but as far north as Perth and west into northern Ireland. But he was working against time: the Empire was in decline and it would not be long until the Romans left Britain, leaving the island prey to instability and invasion. It was also difficult for missionaries to administer such a large area, with the result that later writers complained of lapses in practice by the converts.

But none of this eclipses the triumph and bravery of Ninian's pioneering missionary work. He died and is said to have been buried at Whithorn, which later became one of the foremost centres of pilgrimage in Scotland.

St John Ogilvie
1579–1615
Catholic martyr

Calvinist to Jesuit John Ogilvie was born in Banffshire, the eldest
son of Walter Ogilvie of Drum. He was raised a Calvinist,
although his mother had been a Catholic. At 13 he set off for a
tour of the Continent where he converted to Catholicism and
studied with the Benedictines before joining the Society of Jesus
at Brunn in Bohemia in 1599. The Jesuits were the shock-troops
of the Catholic Church's Counter-Reformation movement. After
11 years' training he was finally ordained in Paris in 1610.

Danger in Scotland Officially, the celebration of Mass in
Scotland was penal, with death for any repetition of the offence.
Against the more cautious instincts of his superiors, Ogilvie
repeatedly pleaded to be sent to his native country, eventually
being allowed to return in 1613. Disguised as a soldier, he crossed
into Scotland and worked in Edinburgh, Renfrew and Glasgow
before he was betrayed and arrested in October 1614.

Imprisonment, torture and martyrdom Ogilvie's trial and imprisonment went on for five more months, when he was interrogated
by Archbishop Spottiswoode of Glasgow. After a preliminary
hearing at which he was found guilty and which should legally
have resulted in his banishment, he was again imprisoned and tortured to the point of death by sleep deprivation for nine nights.
Attempts were made to persuade him to reveal the names of secret
Catholics and to convert him, and he was tried a second time.
Despite conducting an able defence, he was sentenced to death
and hanged at the Tolbooth at Glasgow Cross on 23 February
1615 before a large crowd; a further sentence of quartering against
him was not carried out by the hangman.

John Ogilvie was beatified in 1926 and canonised in 1976. He is
Scotland's only post-Reformation saint.

Margaret Oliphant
1828–97
Writer

Impetus to write Margaret Wilson was born in Wallyford in Midlothian. By the time she was 16 her prodigious writing talent manifested itself in her first novel. She married her cousin, Francis Oliphant, a stained-glass designer, in 1852, and by the time of his death from TB seven years later she had two children, was pregnant with a third and was £1000 in debt. Such an spur would in itself have been enough to ensure her continued literary output, but writing was a compulsion, not a matter of choice for her: 'I must work or die,' she was later to tell her publisher, a prophetic choice of words from one who was to insist on correcting the proofs of her final book on her deathbed.

Tragic family life As well as supporting her own family, Margaret also took on the burden of providing for her extended family. Willie, her brother, was a helpless drunk who had once tried to pass off a piece of her work as his own; she sent him to Italy and maintained him until his death in 1885. She supported her other brother, Frank, a bankrupt, and paid for his family's education. Margaret's own family did not fare well: three of her children died in infancy; her daughter died of gastric fever at the age of 11; and her two sons also predeceased her, dying in young adulthood, like their father, from TB. With such a tragic personal history, it is not surprising that Margaret's literary concerns in the last 20 years of her life turned increasingly to the supernatural.

Her work Her output was immense: 93 novels, over 30 short stories, biographies, histories, reviews, essays and articles. Although her work has been out of print for some time, more of her fiction is becoming available once more, most notably her famous *Chronicles of Carlingford* series of novels of English manners, and her work is an entertaining and rewarding read.

Oor Wullie
First appeared in 1934
Cartoon character

Place in Scottish society As a familiar figure from childhood, Oor Wullie appeals to a craving for the comforting in the psyche of most Scottish adults. A wee boy with spiky hair, dressed in black dungarees and seated on his bucket, Wullie has for years opened and closed the comic strip bearing his name. His pastimes have an idyllic appeal: racing in his cartie, camping with his friends, dookin' for apples at Hallowe'en and staying up for the bells to eat black bun and shortie at Hogmanay. Good-natured, mischievous and wily, Wullie has represented the archetypal Scottish boy, untouched by the upheavals of 20th-century society. Together with The Broons, Wullie has appeared in D. C. Thomson's *Sunday Post*, itself that most archetypal of Scottish newspapers, for years.

The artist's genius Yet despite their often anachronistic storylines, the older Wullie stories are a joy to read. This is due in no small measure to their original artist, Dudley D. Watkins, an illustrator of true genius. Watkins was English; a native of Nottingham, he studied at the city's art school and worked for Boots the Chemist before coming to Dundee to work for Thomson. Although he was the first Thomson artist to be allowed to sign his name, a signature was not needed to identify his distinctive style, visible in characters he worked on and who included Biffo the Bear, Desperate Dan and Lord Snooty; all came to life through a delightful and priceless mastery of touch, facial expression and body movement. Gifted artists have carried on Watkins' work since his death at the early age of 62, but none has quite managed to match his exquisite talent.

Mungo Park
1771–1806
Explorer

Medicine and botany training   Mungo Park was born on a farm at Foulshields near Selkirk, the seventh of 13 children. At the age of 15 years he was apprenticed to a local surgeon. The connection was to prove a fruitful one: as well as gaining a grounding in medicine, Mungo would also marry the doctor's daughter and travel abroad with his son on the last of his expeditions. In 1789 he went to Edinburgh University where he studied botany and qualified in medicine, then took himself off to London.

First African adventures   Through his brother-in-law Park gained powerful friends who shared his interest in botany. One of these friends proposed him for a trip being planned by the African Association, a body set up to further exploration on the continent, to plot the course of the Niger. In May 1795 he set off, and sailed 200 miles up the Gambia River before making landfall at Pisania where he immediately contracted malaria and was laid up for five months. His trip from Pisania inland lasted eight months; during it he suffered robbery several times and even imprisonment, eventually escaping only with the clothes he stood in and his pocket compass which he had cleverly hidden in the sand to prevent its being taken. He tried to carry on, but having no money to buy food he was forced to turn back. En route he fell ill again and was cared for by a native man. Worn out, he eventually reached Falmouth in December 1777.

Fame at home   In 1779 Park published an account of his adventures, *Travels in the Interior Districts of Africa*. The book fed the public appetite for information on the dark continent, and Park's extraordinary tales and his simple narrative style made it an immediate success and its author a celebrity. It went to three editions in one year and even inspired a popular song. Park returned to the

Borders where he married, started a family, set up as a physician and gathered about him talented friends, including Walter **Scott**. But he could not settle at home, and when he was asked to join a government-sponsored expedition to the Niger he found the call irresistible.

Second fateful expedition In January 1805 the party set off, their numbers boosted by a troop of soldiers sent along to protect them. Four months after their arrival in Africa three-quarters of the group were dead of malaria, and by October Park's brother-in-law, whom he nursed personally for three months, had died, too. The remaining little band of four built a boat to sail down the Niger, plotting its course as they went, and Park sent a letter to his family and to the Government swearing to accomplish his task or die in the attempt. He was never seen or heard from again.

His final days It was not until 1812 that a native guide discovered the party's last movements. They had been ambushed by local natives and in the fight that followed all except one native oarsman had drowned. Neither Park's body nor his journals were ever found. His wife and four children received £4000 from the Government. (Sadly, Park's son also died in Africa in an attempt to find out more about what had happened to his father.) He was one of a line of Scottish explorers of Africa, including **Livingstone** and **Bruce**, whose courageous lives fed the clamour for heroes.

William Paterson
1658–1719
Founder of the Bank of England

Little-known early life William Paterson was born at Tinwald but not much is known of his early years. Glamorous accounts state that he lived in the West Indies as a missionary for years before spectacularly changing allegiances to become a buccaneer. He certainly traded with the West Indies while living in London, and enjoyed a high reputation in financial circles by 1690.

Bank of England scheme It is for his establishment of the Bank of England that Paterson's name survives. In 1691 he devised a scheme to let the Government borrow at good rates of interest; lenders would be part of the Company of the Bank of England. It was adopted four years later and Paterson became a director, but he resigned in 1696 after falling out with colleagues.

Darien disaster He returned to Scotland to promote the scheme to establish a Scottish colony at Darien in Panama, then perceived as a potentially great commercial centre. Paterson's backing meant the plan received wide support, and despite early problems, including, ominously, the opposition of major European powers, embezzlement and administrative difficulties, the first lot of settlers, including Paterson, sailed out in 1698. In the event the scheme was a disaster, and the disease-ridden climate saw off most of the colonists, including his wife and son. He returned, broken, with the other survivors, in 1699.

Later ventures He was a notable supporter of the union with England in 1707, and was elected to the first British parliament. But the Darien venture had left him relatively poor, and he supported himself by teaching until he was awarded £18,000 indemnity for his losses in 1715. He again distinguished himself in financial circles when he proposed the scheme for Walpole's Sinking Fund to consolidate and convert the National Debt.

Allan Pinkerton
1819–1884
Founder of the Pinkerton Detective Agency

Chartist activities   Allan Pinkerton was born in Glasgow, the son of a policeman. He was a cooper to trade, and a Chartist. His political activities were such that he went into hiding to avoid arrest. At 23 he emigrated to the US, settling in Dundee, Illinois.

The Pinkerton Agency   After his success in uncovering a local counterfeiting ring he was appointed deputy sheriff, first in Dundee then Chigaco where in 1852 he formed his own group of young and morally upright detectives. Their fame grew after they scored a series of major successes in solving train robberies.

Their successes   One of Pinkerton's most spectacular feats was foiling an assasination attempt against President-elect Abraham Lincoln on his way by train to his inauguration. He headed the US secret service during the Civil War (1861–65), organising spying missions into the Confederacy. With Pinkerton's political beliefs it was not surprising that he should be a fervent abolitionist, and his Chicago home was a station on the Underground Railroad for those fleeing slavery in the south.

The Molly Maguires   His agency's most famous triumph was the breaking up in the 1870s of the Pennsylvania operations of the Molly Maguires, a secret society set up to protect poor Irish immigrants. In Pennsylvania the society had become proactive and criminal, operating through intimidation and murder, but evidence against the leaders was lacking. Pinkerton's plan sent one of his Irish detectives to work in the coal mines where the society was based and infiltrate its organisation. The man was so convincing that he became an official of one of the most notorious lodges, and gathered evidence to secure the arrest, conviction and, in some cases, the execution of members.

After Pinkerton's death his sons carried on his agency's work.

Duke of Queensberry
1724–1810
Rake

Notoriety William Douglas, third Earl of March and fourth Duke of Queensberry, was born in Peebles. His claims to fame were his joint passions for gambling, horse racing and womanising.

Passion for gambling Old Q, as he was known to friends, was a horse-racing expert. He bought a house overlooking the course at Newmarket and maintained his own stables, with jockeys who raced in his own scarlet colours. Unlike many racing enthusiasts, he was also very lucky gambler and won large sums of money from several eminent people. But horses were not the only subject of his wagers: he once bet that he could send a letter 50 miles in one hour, and had it sewn into a ball which was then thrown from one person to another in a human chain across the entire distance.

The Hellfire Club Old Q was a member of the notorious Hellfire Club, whose motto was, 'Do what you please; dare to despise convention.' However, he had a falling-out with a fellow member, John Wilkes, which ended, oddly, in Queensberry's prosecuting him for obscenity in 1763. Wilkes had written *Essay on Woman*, an obscene parody of Pope's *Essay on Man*, for the delight of his fellow club members. But Wilkes was expelled from the club when he dressed up a monkey as Satan and set it loose during one of the club's black masses, causing terror and hysteria among the 'celebrants'. By way of revenge, Queensberry and others named Wilkes as the author of the obscene publication.

Sexual promiscuity Like many of his fellow club members, Queensberry's sexual habits were promiscuous and scandalous. He pursued very young women, especially adolescents, with a single mindedness bordering on obsession. His particular penchant was for opera singers, and he was once the subject of a paternity suit brought by an opera singer. So, he later discovered, was one of his friends; in fact, despite both having paid out large sums, neither man was the father.

Eccentric habits Queensberry was considered eccentric in his personal habits: he ate carefully, made sure to get enough sleep every night and bathed regularly in milk, all in order to maintain his sexual potency. His doctor, the former personal physician of Louis XV, was paid on a daily basis for keeping his master alive and healthy; his wages were to cease on the day his employer died. Even into old age, Queensberry's desires – if not his potency – remained, and he would sit above the porch of his Piccadilly house ogling young women in the street.

Universal opprobrium Queensberry was almost universally reviled, often in public: William Wordsworth called him 'Degenerate Douglas', and Robert **Burns** also criticised him in verse for chopping down thousands of trees on his estates to make money to pay off his gambling debts. This method of payment, or perhaps his long-term betting luck, seemed to work: by the time he died, his personal fortune was over one million pounds.

Henry Raeburn
1756–1823
Artist

Orphaned Born in Stockbridge, Henry Raeburn was the son of a Borders manufacturer. He was an orphan by the age of six, and was cared for by his brother, William, 12 years his senior.

Artistic training Henry became an apprentice goldsmith at 16, but his artistic talent was already evident in watercolour miniatures, and his master introduced him to David Martin, the Edinburgh society portrait painter of the day. Raeburn learned much from Martin, although their relationship later cooled. He took naturally to working in oils, and his reputation grew.

Marriage In 1778 an attractive woman came to be painted whom Raeburn recognised from one of his sketching expeditions, when he had been so struck by her that he had included her in his sketch. Within a few months the two were married. She was several years older, the Scots widow of a French nobleman and the mother of three young children. She was also personally wealthy, and she and Raeburn enjoyed a happy marriage.

Reputation established Raeburn went to Rome with his family to study from 1785 to 1787 on the advice of Joshua Reynolds. This experience complemented his natural talent, allowing him to become the foremost Scottish portrait painter. He lived in Edinburgh from 1787 until his death, and during that time painted the most rich and powerful figures in the land, including **Cockburn**, **Hume**, **Boswell**, **Smith**, **Braxfield** and **Scott**.

His work He was a personally genial man who painted for the love of it, declaring painting the most delightful thing in the world. He painted straight onto canvas with a vigorous style, imaginative colour and positive brushwork. He always began with the features, which he considered most important, and his paintings expose his subjects' character as well as appearance.

Allan Ramsay
1713–1784
Artist

Early talent The son of Allan Ramsay the poet, Allan was the eldest of eight children of whom only three outlived their parents. He was born in Edinburgh and showed a precocious talent for drawing which was encouraged by his father. At 20 he moved to London to study with, among others, Hogarth, who was impressed by his talent. In 1736 he left for the Continent and, after being almost shipwrecked at Pisa, arrived in Rome where he stayed studying and working for almost three years.

Royal patronage On his return he established himself as one of the most successful and talented portrait painters, and by the time he moved to London in 1762 he was a rich man whose reputation was secure. This was emphasised by his appointment as George III's portrait painter five years later, and the king's tendency to give away portraits of himself and Queen Charlotte as gifts meant that Ramsay was never short of royal commissions.

Other interests Ramsay has been recognised, with Hogarth, as one of the founders of a new school of portraiture in Britain. His style changed after his move to London, to a more subtle, natural style. Perhaps because of this he is regarded as one of the finest portrait painters of women. But his interests never lay solely in painting: he was an intellectual who cultivated the society of some of the foremost minds of his day. He established the Select Society in Edinburgh in 1754, whose members included **Monboddo**, **Hume** and **Smith**; he corresponded with Voltaire and Rousseau; and he was a member of Dr Johnson's circle.

Retirement and death In 1773 Ramsay broke his arm in an accident in a fire drill at his home, and thereafter went into semi-retirement. He moved to Italy in his later years and died at Dover on his way home during a bout of homesickness.

John Reith
1889–1971
Broadcasting pioneer

Upbringing   John Reith was born in 1889 at Stonehaven in Kincardineshire. He was the son of a minister, and the values which were inculcated into him as a child were enduring, colouring not only his own outlook but also those of the broadcasting organisation which was essentially his creation.

War service   Reith served an engineering apprenticeship in Glasgow and quickly volunteered for service in the First World War. He was invalided out of the army after a sniper's bullet hit him in the head in an encounter which left him with a livid scar across his face. In 1922 he applied for and got – possibly because of his engineering background – the newly created post of general manager of the British Broadcasting Company, to be in charge of a staff of four people.

Establishing the BBC   Reith was a towering and assertive personality who in many ways was the archetypal dry, cerebral, moral Scot. From the first he dominated the infant company, stamping his influence on its every action. He was aware of the huge potential for influence which lay in broadcasting, and was adamant that the company must remain absolutely impartial and should not be used as the tool of any government. His first real confrontation came during the 1926 General Strike, when he refused to allow Winston Churchill to use the BBC for anti-strike propaganda. He worked successfully to take the BBC out of the commercial sphere and have it established under royal charter as a public corporation, and in 1927 he became the first Director-General of the new British Broadcasting Corporation, a post he held until 1938. His control during those years was autocratic, and he expected standards of behaviour and decorum from his staff which today seem extraordinary – radio announcers wearing dinner jackets and a bias against employing divorcés were some of the more extreme examples of his determination to impart dignity, respect and a moral sense throughout the corporation. Although Reith worked with the BBC for only 16 years, the influence he wielded was huge, and he was responsible for the organisation's move into public service broadcasting, which endures to the present day. The high standards he imparted to the BBC, with what he saw as its power to explain impartially and fairly, and thereby influence society

for the good, were central in building up the corporation's reputation which, to a large extent, it has managed to retain.

Later work Reith left the BBC in 1938 to manage Imperial Airways. Although he had a disparate succession of jobs, he never again found one so suited to his talents. He became MP for Southampton, and served as Minister of Works and Buildings for two years during the war. However, he and Churchill had never got on, and Reith was deprived of his cabinet post in 1942, a move which left him bitter. Reith worked in the war effort and held a variety of posts, including that of chairman of the Commonwealth Telecommunications Board, after the war. He returned to Scotland to live only in the last year of his life, and died in Edinburgh. In 1948 the BBC instituted the series of Reith Lectures in his honour.

Robert I, the Bruce
1274–1329
King of Scots

Lineage Robert Bruce was born of a Scots–Norman father and a mother descended from the Celtic earls of Galloway. The Bruce family had asserted their hereditary claim to the Scottish throne since 1286; so, too, had the Balliols, and the bitter rivalry between these two families had important consequences both for Robert Bruce and for Scotland.

Wavering allegiance As a young man, Bruce proved himself to be more pragmatic than patriotic. John Balliol was chosen by Edward I of England to fill the vacant Scottish throne in 1292, and the English king used the event to press his claim to over-lordship of the Scots. In common with the majority of the Scottish nobility, Bruce gave at least nominal allegiance to the English king. However, when Balliol rebelled in 1296, the Bruces became much more supportive of the English king, fighting for him in the hope of advancing their own cause. This vacillating allegiance continued, as Bruce at first participated in the **Wallace** rebellion in 1297, but then served Edward from 1302.

Sacrilege in the church In 1306, however, Bruce decided to put himself at the head of a revived national independence movement to press his claim for the throne. He tried to win over to his cause John Comyn of Badenoch, a former Guardian of Scotland who was now main represener of the Balliol interests. A personal feud also existed between the two men – in 1299 Comyn had publicly grabbed Bruce around the throat during an argument. Putting personal and family enmity aside for the national good was too much to ask, and at a meeting between the two at the Greyfriars' church in Dumfries the feuds resurfaced, and after a violent quarrel Bruce and his supporters murdered Comyn. Bruce was later excommunicated for the murder.

Revenge of Edward of England He was hurriedly crowned King of Scots at Scone, an act which roused the ageing Edward I to a savage revenge: he attempted to eradicate the Bruce family, executing the men with butchery and imprisoning the women. He took his army north, and although he died before he reached the border, his hatred of the Scots was immortalised on his tombstone with the words *Edward Primus, Scotorum Malleus* (Hammer of the Scots).

The long road back Robert's forces were scattered and the king and his loyal supporters were fugitives. It was said to be at this low point of his fortunes that, sheltering in a cave, he learned the effectiveness of endurance from the example of a spider struggling again and again to climb a wall to build her web. In 1307 Robert began the long haul of driving the English, now ruled by the weak Edward II, out of the country. He waged a remarkable campaign of guerrilla warfare which, over the next seven years, reduced the number of English strongholds in Scotland to only two: Berwick and Stirling. These victories eased the doubts of many Scots nobles who had questioned Robert's ability to be a national leader.

Bannockburn Confidence in his ability was greatly reinforced by his greatest victory, at Bannockburn in June 1314. Against a much larger and better equipped force, Robert's superior tactics and his disposition of his forces won the day; the English army was decimated, losing three-quarters of its 20,000-strong force, and Edward fled the field in disgrace. One chronicler called it 'the most lamentable defeat which an English army ever suffered'. An example of Robert's bravery, and perhaps also of his recklessness, is well illustrated in an incident the night before the battle proper. An English knight, Humphrey de Bohun, challenged the Scots' champion to fight in single combat before the battle, and the king insisted on meeting the challenge himself. The men, both on horseback, faced one another before their armies. de Bohun rode a large, heavy, unmanoeuvrable charger, needed to bear the weight of the armour he wore. By contrast, Robert wore light armour and had a much smaller, nimbler mount. He stood motionless in the face of de Bohun's thundering charge until the last moment when, pulling his horse's head quickly to one side, he turned, rose up in the stirrups and buried his battleaxe in the passing English knight's skull to the cheers of the Scots army. Robert, chastised by his shocked lieutenants for his recklessness, merely lamented the loss of his good axe.

Declaration of Arbroath The following year Robert was unanimously confirmed by Parliament, and a detailed Act of succession was agreed. The war with England was continued intermittently, waged largely by James **Douglas** and Robert's nephew, Thomas Randolph, until Scottish independence was recognised in 1328 in the Treaty of Northampton. Bannockburn had been a turning point, and Scotland was never again subject to the overlordship of England. Other European countries recognised Scottish independence, but one of the most important was recognition by the papacy and the lifting of Robert's excommunication after the 1320 Declaration of Arbroath, a letter from the Scots nobles to the pope which has stood as a poignant declaration of Scottish patriotism and independence: 'While there exist a hundred of us we will never submit to England. For we fight not for glory, wealth, or honour, but for that liberty which no virtuous man lays down but with his life.'

Robert in peacetime For a man who had made his name as a superb general, Robert proved to be a surprisingly successful king in peacetime. He reasserted royal authority throughout the realm, even managing to reconcile the factions which had lost out in the succession battles of the 1290s. He instigated legal reforms, and his care of the rights of the ordinary people earned him respect and the affectionate name of 'good King Robert'. He died at Cardross in 1329, ravaged, it is said, by leprosy, apparently contracted during the hardships of his life on the run.

His importance Although not initially a patriot, once Robert came to the fore he pursued his aims selflessly and with brilliant success. Scotland owed its continuing independence to him and he stands arguably as the single most important figure in Scottish history.

James Robertson-Justice
1905–1975
Actor

James Robertson-Justice was born in Wigtownshire and educated at Bonn University, where he completed his PhD.

Early career A multi-talented individual, he turned his hand to many jobs before settling on acting fairly late in life. He taught, wrote, sold insurance, steered a barge and dug sewers. He was also a journalist with Reuters News Agency, and worked in Canada for the British United Press. He was said to be able to speak 10 languages, although he himself claimed only five – French, German, Italian, Dutch and Gaelic.

Politics and war service Robertson-Justice also saw active service in the 1930s and '40s. A committed socialist (he stood unsuccessfully for Labour in the 1950 general election), he went to Spain during the Civil War to serve in the International Brigades, and was an officer in the Royal Navy during the Second World War.

'Discovered' He was acting as MC in a music-hall act when he was 'spotted' by a film director and given a small part in the film *Fiddlers Three* (1944). Other Ealing films, including *Scott of the Antarctic* and *Whisky Galore* followed, and in 1951 he left for Hollywood for several years, working on films such as *Moby Dick*.

The Doctor films But his most distinctive role was as Sir Lancelot Sprat, imperious and terrifying medical knight in the series of films which began with *Doctor in the House* in 1954. He fitted the part so well that most of his subsequent roles were in the same comic vein, although he did make occasional departures into more unexpected areas, such as in the Roger Vadim film *Le Repos du Guerrier* playing a victim of the charms of Brigitte Bardot.

Conservation interests He was also an active conservationist and a Fellow of the Zoological Society. He trained and flew falcons, and invented a rocket-propelled net to catch birds for marking.

Michael Scott
c. 1175–c. 1234
Wizard

Education Not much is known of Michael Scott's early life, although it is assumed that he came from a Borders family. He was educated at Oxford, Paris and Padua. Between 1209 and 1220 he studied at the Moorish city of Toledo in Spain, translating works by Aristotle and Averroës, among others.

Astrologer of the Holy Roman Empire Scott joined Emperor Frederick the Great's glittering court at Palermo, known as 'Stupor Mundi', 'Wonder of the World'. The emperor gathered around him the most learned scholars of the known world and Scott, with a suitable outlet for his talents, became court astrologer. Through his Arabic translations, many works which had been lost to or were unknown in Christendom were reintroduced and discovered. In 1223 he was offered the archbishopric of Cashel by the pope, but refused on the grounds that he did not know Irish. Scott's own interests lay more in astrology and the occult, including alchemy, sorcery, physiognomy and prophesy.

Powers His reputed powers were respected and feared. He was said to fly through the air on an invisible horse, and sail on a demon ship. He foretold the emperor's death, and foresaw that his own would come from a blow to the head by a stone of two ounces or less; consequently he fashioned a metal helmet which he wore constantly. It is said that he lifted the helmet, mockingly, during the consecration of a Mass and was instantly struck dead by a small stone which fell from the roof of the church.

Fame Scott was known throughout Europe: he appeared among the enchanters in the eighth circle of Hell in Dante's *Inferno*; he was mentioned by Boccaccio; and Walter **Scott** wrote about him. His spell books and books of knowledge still existed at the end of the 16th century, but their whereabouts now is unknown.

Walter Scott
1771–1832
Writer

Legal background Scott is Scotland's most prolific and, some claim, best writer, and a founder of the historical novel. He was born in Edinburgh, the ninth child of a lawyer. As an infant he contracted polio which left him permanently lame in his right leg. After Edinburgh University he served his legal apprenticeship in his father's firm before being called to the Bar in 1792.

Literary beginnings From an early age Scott was interested in ballads, and in 1802 his own volume, *The Border Minstrelsy*, was published by Kelso printer, James Ballantyne, in what became a long and ultimately disastrous association. Although a successful lawyer, Scott continued to write ballads and poetry and made enough money to buy a country house at Abbotsford in 1812.

The *Waverley* novels The following year Scott rediscovered in a drawer a manuscript for a novel, *Waverley*, which he had left aside several years before. He decided it was good enough to finish, published it and enjoyed instant success. A series of these novels followed, all successful, and all anonymously published until 1827 – Scott evidently felt that his position in society would be compromised by earning money from writing.

Society figure Scott enjoyed a high social profile and entertained a host of famous people, from Washington Irving to Thomas Moore, and Humphry Davy to William Wordsworth. He was also well received at court, and attended the coronation of George IV in 1821. He was the prime organiser behind the king's visit to Scotland in 1822 when the leaders of Highland society came bedecked in a tartan extravaganza of kitsch and ahistorical finery.

His collections Scott was financially extravagant, expanding Abbotsford and buying land. He also added to his private collection of oddments from Scottish history, with items ranging from

Prince **Charles'** quaich to an oatcake taken from the sporran of a Highlander who fought at Culloden. One of his later acquisitions was to have been a glass from which George IV had drunk on his visit to Edinburgh. Scott begged to have it, and put it in his back trouser pocket for safe keeping; unfortunately, it was sat upon in a moment of forgetfulness.

Writing himself to the grave Scott's management of his finances had been going wrong for some time but finally, in 1826, the whole precarious structure fell down around him. He enjoyed an extravagant lifestyle and had invested badly in Ballantyne's publishing ventures. He found himself £100,000 in debt but pledged to work until all his creditors were paid off. The flurry of writing activity which resulted threatened his health, which had never been stable for long periods. (On one blackly comic occasion in 1819, when Scott had been expected to die and his family were gathered around his sickbed, the Earl of Buchan tried to force his way into the room to cheer Scott up with details of the spectacular funeral he had arranged for him.) Much of this later work was of inferior quality, written merely to pay off his debts – which he largely achieved – but by 1830 his health was broken. The Government offered him the use of a frigate, and he set off in 1831 for a holiday in the Mediterranean. He died at Abbotsford shortly after his return, and is buried at Dryburgh Abbey.

Alexander Selkirk
1676–1721
Castaway and model for *Robinson Crusoe*

Restless nature The seventh son of John Selcraig, a Largo shoe-maker, Alexander Selkirk – a name he later adopted – was a high-spirited young man. He ran away to sea in 1695, possibly after a citation to appear before the local kirk session, the church court, for 'indecent behaviour' in church. He returned to Largo for a time and made another appearance in the kirk session registers in 1701, this time for quarrelling with his brothers.

Marooned in the South Seas He left again, and by 1703 had joined a privateer. In 1704, as the ship was at the uninhabited South Pacific island of Juan Fernandez, Selkirk quarrelled with the captain and demanded to be put ashore. When he was landed he changed his mind but unfortunately the captain did not, and the ship left without him. Selkirk was distraught, but adapted quickly. He built huts and hunted goats for food. When his powder ran out he learned to climb and chase the goats to catch them. He dodged the attentions of a passing Spanish ship which fired at him. Finally in 1809 he was rescued by a privateer whose attention he attracted with a fire. He resumed his privateering activities, finally arriving back in Britain almost two years later.

Fame Several accounts, including his own, were published of his adventures. (Defoe based *Robinson Crusoe*, published in 1719, on these.) He returned to Largo a famous man in 1712 but declared that he wanted to be a recluse, and built a cave-like dwelling in his father's garden. But his determination on the solitary life evidently wavered, as he persuaded a young local woman to elope with him. He ruined the poor woman by not marrying her, then abandoning her to return to the sea. Selkirk eventually married a widow in 1720, the year before his death from fever while serving as a lieutenant in the Royal Navy.

Patrick Sellar
1780–1851
Sutherland factor during the Clearances

Patrick Sellar was born at Westfield in Morayshire. He was educated in the law at Edinburgh, and on his return north was employed by the first Duke of Sutherland as his factor.

The Clearances In the wake of the Jacobite rebellion of Prince **Charles** Edward Stuart in 1745, the British Government savagely suppressed the Highlands, actively trying to break down the ancient social ties of clanship and encouraging clan chiefs to clear clansmen off the lands. Consequently, many chiefs treated clan lands and those living on them as they saw fit. The Duke of Sutherland was one such who cleared people from clan lands which their families had worked for generations, to the coast, where they could, he decided, farm and fish also.

Ruthlessness and brutality As factor, Sellar was in the front line of those whose duty was to evict and move clan members off the land. Contemporary descriptions of Sellar's burning families out of their homes make pitiful reading, but he considered those with whom he dealt to be less than human. In a description whose essence is horribly reminiscent of anti-Jewish Nazi propaganda of the 1930s, he compared the Highlanders and the American Indians: 'both live in turf cabins in common with the brutes; both are singular for patience, courage, cunning and address. Both are most virtuous where least in contact with men in a civilised State, and both are fast sinking under the baneful effects of ardent spirits.' He conducted his job with such enthusiasm and brutality that he was eventually tried in court for oppression in 1816, although he was acquitted. He later became a sheep farmer on the cleared land. Even today, Sellar's name is still notorious and is synonymous with the Clearances.

James Young Simpson
1811–1870
Pioneer of anaesthesia

Poverty and precocious talent James Young Simpson was born in
Bathgate, the youngest of seven sons of the local baker and his
wife. He was an academically talented boy and when he was 15 his
widower father and six brothers saved money to send him to
Edinburgh University. He studied medicine, although his distress
at patients' suffering was almost enough to make him abandon the
subject in favour of law. He graduated in 1832, and his genius was
such that by 1839, although only 28 years old, he was appointed
to the chair of midwifery in Edinburgh.

Discovery of chloroform Throughout Simpson's life, the allevia-
tion of physical pain and suffering was his major preoccupation.
He was particularly concerned to find a means of sending patients
to sleep to avoid the worst agonies of childbirth and the terrors of
surgery. In 1846 he was excited by new trials with ether in
America, but after experimentation concluded that it was not
ideal: large amounts were often needed, which could be haz-
ardous, and it could irritate the lungs. Chloroform was undergo-
ing similar trials in France in 1847, and by November Simpson
was ready to test this. He and his two assistants, Drs Duncan and
Keith, sat around a table with a bottle of chloroform between
them. All inhaled the chloroform simultaneously through their
handkerchiefs, and within a minute the three fell unconscious to
the floor. Two weeks later Simpson was using the anaesthetic in
his practice at Edinburgh Infirmary.

Battle against superstition However, the religious authorities considered sleep-inducing drugs to be dangerous to religion, morals
and health, and many considered it unnatural to alleviate the pain
of childbirth. Simpson fought a bitter battle against them, saying
'every operation without it is just a piece of the most deliberate

and cold-blooded cruelty.' The use of anaesthetic only gradually gained acceptance; the first baby born to a mother with benefit of the drug was named Anaesthesia in its honour. It finally gained full respectability when Queen Victoria took it during the birth of Prince Leopold, her sixth child, in 1853.

Unaffected by success Simpson was showered with honours from all over Europe and America, and was made a baronet in 1866, the first practicing Scottish doctor to be so recognised. However, he continued in his own practice in Edinburgh, ministering to both rich and poor. As well as his championing of chloroform, Simpson made other noted advances, particularly in the fields of investigation, diagnosis and treatment in obstetrics and gynaecology. He was concerned with hospital mortality rates, and advocated patient isolation as a way of reducing them, but although he saw the spread of infection as one of the causes, ironically he quarrelled with Joseph Lister over the practice of antisepsis.

Family Simpson died relatively early, of angina. His family were asked, but refused, to allow his body to be buried in Westminster Abbey; instead, he was buried, in a public funeral, at Warriston Cemetery in Edinburgh. His wife, Jessie, lived for only a few weeks after his death. Of their nine children, only four survived them.

Mary Slessor
1848–1915
Missionary

Importance David **Livingstone**'s is the name which immediately comes to mind when one thinks of Scots missionaries, but in bringing practical benefits to humanity he was far outstripped by Mary Slessor.

Early life Mary was born in Aberdeen, one of five children of a shoemaker. When she was 10 the family moved to Dundee where Mary worked in the jute mills. She was a member of the United Presbyterian Church, and in the early 1870s her imagination was captured by Livingstone's exploits in Africa. She applied to the Foreign Mission Board for work as a teacher in Calabar in West Africa, finally setting out in 1876.

An unconventional missionary Mary's behaviour on arrival scandalised genteel missionary society: she mixed and socialised with natives; she walked inland to meet them; and, worse, she cut her hair short and wore light clothing, leaving off corsets, shoes, hats and veils. Her time in Africa was marked by frequent conflict with the authorities. Within a few years she was transferred from the base station at Duke Town to the more distant Old Town, later moving even further inland to Okoyong at her own request.

Dispelling barbarism The society Mary encountered in Africa would be shocking today; to a young Victorian woman it must have been beyond belief. But Mary's great assets were adaptability and strength of will. Once, soon after her arrival, she almost literally stumbled across a brutal ritualistic rape in a village. Infuriated, she waded into the assailants wielding her umbrella, breaking heads and jabbing bare flesh with the metal point. The 'warriors' quickly dispersed. She persuaded local people that the birth of twins was not a sign of coupling with devils, but of male virility and a cause for celebration, not infanticide. (Mary's persuasion took some time, and in the meantime she acquired a large adopted family, many of them twins.) She worked to end the practice of propitiatory human sacrifice in times of sickness. But it was with the lot of women and children that Mary was most concerned, and she saved many from enslavement or terrible death. She ended the practice of slaughtering the wife and slaves of rich men who died, and saved orphans from being thrown into the graves of their parents. She ridiculed before an entire village one powerful old man who had locked up his young wives to prevent their running away. Later, when she was appointed vice-consul in Okoyong, she presided over the native court where it was said that no woman ever lost a case under her.

Personal life When Mary was 43 she was wooed by a 25-year-old missionary, Charles Morrison, who fell deeply in love with her. They became engaged, but the authorities refused him permission to join Mary at Okoyong. His health suffered and he was sent home to recover, but in a short time was dead of a broken heart.

Her legacy Mary set up churches, schools and hospitals all over her area of West Africa. In her later years she was almost crippled by arthritis, but refused to leave her post. She died in 1915, having done invaluable work to alleviate suffering and raise the local people from the mire of savagery.

Samuel Smiles
1812–1904
Social reformer

Medical training The son of a paper-maker, Samuel Smiles was one of 11 children. He graduated in medicine from Edinburgh in 1832 and set up practice in Haddington, but in 1838 he sold up, having decided that it was not the career for him.

Reforming journalist While travelling in the north of England later that year he applied for and got the vacant post of editor of the radical *Leeds Times*. He stayed with the paper for four years, eventually resigning to concentrate on lecturing and freelance journalism to give full rein to his radical and reforming instincts, which included support for household suffrage, state education, public libraries and the anti-Corn Law movement.

'Do thou likewise' In 1840 Smiles met railway pioneer George Stephenson. It was a seminal event for him: like so many Victorians, the new transport captured his imagination, and he would later work in railway enterprise for 20 years. Stephenson's death in 1848 prompted Smiles to write his biography, published in 1857. He followed it up two years later with a collection of biographies of contemporary men of achievement, entitled *Self-Help*. This book was the Bible of the Victorian society, with its admonition to readers to follow in these achievers' progressive, trail-blazing footsteps. It was an instant success, ultimately selling over 250,000 copies in Britain, with translations into other languages. Smiles reworked the theme, milking it dry with a succession of similar works bearing such deeply off-putting titles as *Thrift, Character, Duty* and *Life and Labour*. He suffered a stroke through overwork in 1871 and took time off to travel through Europe where he was well received by, among others, Garibaldi. He continued to write biographies, with subjects including James **Watt** and, in *Lives of the Engineers*, Thomas **Telford**.

Adam Smith
1723–1790
Economist and philosopher

Eventful childhood Adam Smith was born in Kirkcaldy, an only child whose father died before he was born. At the age of three he was abducted by gypsies before being quickly rescued. Friends in his home town included the **Adam** brothers.

Diverse talents Smith was educated at Glasgow and Oxford, which he disliked and where he was censured after being caught reading **Hume**'s *Treatise of Human Nature*. His literary interests led him to set up in Edinburgh as a freelance lecturer in 1748, combining talks on literature with other subjects which interested him, including philosophy and economics. His success was so outstanding that he was offered the vacant chair of logic at Glasgow University in 1751. The following year he became professor of moral philosophy.

Glasgow years Smith called the years he spent in Glasgow the happiest of his life. As well as enjoying the friendship of Hume's circle of Edinburgh intellectuals, he socialised with Glasgow merchants who gave him the benefits of their practical knowledge; he, in turn, converted them to support for free trade. In 1759 he published his *Theory of Moral Sentiments*, expounding the theory of sympathy as a temper to human selfishness and a means to happiness. It was received with acclaim from, among others, Edmund Burke, and it established his reputation as a philosopher. It also led to a two-year appointment as tutor to the young Duke of Buccleuch and his brother on their two-year European tour in 1764. In France he met Voltaire and other prominent thinkers.

The Wealth of Nations In 1766 Smith settled in Kirkcaldy to work on his masterpiece, *The Wealth of Nations*, which was finally published in 1776. It examined freedom of economic association – *laissez-faire* – and its consequences for nations and politics. The

book founded political economy as a subject. It was instantly influential and successful, and has never been out of print. At a dinner which Smith later attended in London, William Pitt insisted that he should be seated first, stating that 'we are all your scholars'. In 1778 Smith was appointed commissioner of customs in Edinburgh and was comfortably enough off to work on his writings. However, most of these were burnt at his own request by his friends and executors Joseph **Black** and James **Hutton** when his health was failing in his final year.

Personality Smith was an affable man, somewhat reserved but fond of socialising, especially with friends at his Sunday evening suppers. His temper, however, was fierce when roused. After Hume, a noted atheist, died in 1776 Smith wrote an account of his peaceful end which scandalised many religious persons. **Scott** told the story that Samuel Johnson particularly was outraged, and called Smith a liar. Smith retorted angrily that Johnson was a brute and a son of a bitch. He was very absent-minded – once abstractedly returning the respectful military-style salute of a porter – and could fall into a reverie even in the company of others. While in Paris, Smith was at the centre of two unrequited love affairs – his own for an English lady and that of a French noblewoman for him. He also had a long-term love affair which ended, and he never married.

George Smith of Glenlivet
1792–1871
Whisky distiller

Glenlivet whisky George Smith was born on a farm at Upper Drumin on the Duke of Gordon's Glenlivet Estate. He was apprentice to a carpenter, but his area of Banffshire was at the centre of the whisky trade, and Smith was soon involved in it.

Legitimate distillery The 1820s saw reform in the whisky industry. Past pressure from English distillers had resulted in a series of draconian taxes against whisky, but these merely drove the trade underground. A new licensing act of 1823 encouraged distillers to take out licences to produce whisky, and the Duke of Gordon, as a prime mover in the reforms, encouraged all his tenants to comply. Several did so, but after threats to their persons and distilleries they gave up. Smith then agreed to license his Glenlivet distillery, a fact which so incensed his still-illegal neighbours that he was obliged to carry a pair of hair-trigger pistols in his belt for his protection. His persistence and obvious financial success eventually carried the day for the pro-licensers. With the help of Andrew Usher, the Edinburgh merchant, Glenlivet became the most popular whisky in the country.

Fighting off competition Smith's son, John Gordon, abandoned law studies in Edinburgh to work in the ever-expanding family business. In 1860 the two set up a new company and built a new distillery at Minmore in Glenlivet. But success brought its own complications: most of the distilleries in the area were cashing in on the success by calling their whiskies Glenlivet. Intervention by the Duke of Gordon failed to work, and after George died John took the case to court, winning a settlement that only his company could use the direct article in their whisky's name; others were to use the name Glenlivet as a hyphenated suffix. The Glenlivet is still one of the most popular whiskies worldwide.

Madeleine Smith
1835–1928
Alleged poisoner

Madeleine Smith was the daughter of a well-to-do Glasgow architect and the accused in one of the most sensational murder trials ever held in a Scottish court.

Fatal attraction In 1855 the lovely Madeleine met and fell in love with Pierre Emile L'Angelier, a clerk from Jersey. Although her father forbade contact, the two enjoyed a passionate and uninhibited affair during which Madeleine wrote to her lover a series of explicit love letters. They seemed keen to marry, but Madeleine's feelings eventually cooled, especially when she was courted by William Minnoch, a richer and more acceptable suitor. She tried to break off the relationship, but L'Angelier threatened to show her father her letters if she ended their affair or saw Minnoch again. In early 1857 Madeleine was recorded as having bought arsenic three times at local chemists' shops, and her lover died a few weeks later. His body was buried, but after five days was exhumed on suspicion. A post-mortem revealed arsenic poisoning and Madeleine was arrested for murder.

Trial for murder Her trial at Edinburgh High Court began on 30 June 1857 and lasted nine days; if found guilty she would face death by public hanging. The trial caused a sensation in Scotland and beyond; people, mostly sympathetic to Madeleine, queued for hours for admittance to the public gallery, and newspapers published up to four editions daily, recording every detail of how she looked and behaved. Madeleine retained an undisturbed composure throughout.

The verdict Victorian middle-class Scotland was scandalised by Madeleine's conduct and more so by her letters which, with their open references to sex, generated great hostility to her when they were read out. But she was brilliantly defended by her lawyer,

John Inglis, the Dean of the Faculty of Advocates, who depicted her as an innocent seduced by a blackmailing blackguard. Also, and more crucially, no evidence emerged during the trial of her having met her lover on the days before his death. The jury took 22 minutes to reach a verdict of 'Not Proven' on the murder charge. The public gallery erupted into cheers, which were taken up by the crowds thronging Parliament Square outside. Inglis sank into his chair and covered his face with his hands. He left the court without acknowledging Madeleine, who received the verdict utterly impassively.

Marriage and friendships Shunned by her family, Madeleine moved to London where she established herself as a society figure; it is believed that she set the fashion of using table mats instead of a tablecloth at the dinner table. In 1861 she was given away by her father at her marriage to William Morris's associate George Wardle. She settled in Bloomsbury and became involved in the socialist movement, befriending, among others, George Bernard Shaw and R. B. **Cunninghame Graham**. George and Lena, as she was now called, had two children but the couple later separated and she emigrated to America in 1916 at the age of 80. There she married again, refusing all offers and inducements from Hollywood to participate in a film of her life. She died of kidney disease in New York aged 92.

Tobias Smollett
1721–1771
Writer

Early life Born at Vale of Leven, Tobias Smollett was the son of a
laird. He studied medicine at Glasgow, but in 1740 set off for
London in search of a producer for his new play, *The Regicide*.
Disgust at his failure resulted in his joining the Navy as a surgeon's
mate. While his ship was stationed at Jamaica Smollett met his
future wife, the Creole daughter of an English planter.

Literary success In 1744 he returned to London to try to find
work as a surgeon, but his aptitude and first preference was always
for writing. His outspokenness, prejudice and vicious turn of
phrase made him particularly suited to political satire. In 1748 he
put his Navy experience to good use in the anonymously published and highly successful *Adventures of Roderick Random*.
Smollett was not slow to capitalise on its success, publishing his
old *Regicide* as 'by the author of Roderick Random' in 1749.
Another novel featuring the same type of unprincipled hero as
Random, *Peregrine Pickle*, was published in 1751.

Travels abroad Smollett dabbled in journalism and medicine for
a few years. As editor of the *Critical Review* from 1756 to 1763,
he spent three months in jail for libel. But his health was not good
– he had TB – and he was advised to take the Continental air. His
unpleasant experiences were recounted in *Travels through France
and Italy*, published in 1766, and led Laurence Sterne to nickname him Smelfungus. His last work was published in the year he
died: *The Expedition of Humphrey Clinker* is a delightful comic
novel and has been his most enduring.

Personal tragedy Smollett was devastated by the death of his
teenage daughter in 1763, a tragedy from which he never fully
recovered. Despite his prejudices against foreign lands, he left for
Italy again when his health worsened, and died at Livorno.

Lord Stair
1619–1695
Judge

James Dalrymple was born in Ayrshire and educated at Glasgow and Edinburgh. His studies were interrupted from 1639 to 1641 by service in the Army of the Covenant, fighting the religious changes imposed by Charles I. He became an advocate in 1648.

His true allegiance During the civil war and Commonwealth Stair served all sides: he was a commissioner sent by the Scots to negotiate terms with Charles II; a Cromwellian commissioner for the administration of justice in Scotland; and finally a judge under the Restoration. The truth was that, unusually for a lawyer, Stair was relatively unconcerned with constitutional politics. His family had a history of support for extreme reformed religion dating from the time of Wycliffe, and the practice of his religion was his primary preoccupation. In the 1670s he and his family supported the Covenanters, now whittled down from the popular and mass movement of the 1630s to a fanatical rump of illegal extremists. This brought them into conflict with **Dundee**. Such was their vehemence that they were suspected of witchcraft by the common people; by the establishment they were simply disliked. In 1681 Stair resigned his judicial post rather than take the oath of the Test Act, requiring adherence to the monarchy and to Protestantism as defined in the 1560 Confession of Faith.

Legal work In 1681 he published *Institutes of the Law of Scotland*. It was the first work to bring the various elements and principles of Scots law together into a single system and treatise, and is one of the most important works on the subject ever produced.

Reward Stair fled to Holland, returning in triumph in 1689 with William of Orange after James VII's deposition. He and his eldest son, John, became William's right-hand men. John was responsible for carrying out the massacre at Glencoe in 1692.

Jock Stein
1922–1985
Football manager

Playing days The greatest football manager Scotland has ever produced, Jock Stein was born at Burnbank. Originally a miner, he was a mediocre player with Albion Rovers and Llanelli before signing for **Celtic** in 1951. He was a success as centre-half, ending his career with the club only after an ankle injury in 1956.

Managerial apprenticeship A spell as Celtic reserve coach ended in 1957 when he left to manage Dunfermline. His unfancied side beat Celtic to win the Scottish Cup in 1961 and went on to make their mark in Europe. A few months with Hibernian in 1965 preceded his appointment as first Protestant manager of Celtic, the originally Irish Catholic club which was then ailing.

His genius Innovative, imaginative, a supreme tactician, an ardent student of the game and an inspired motivator, Stein acquired messianic status. He was a devoted believer in attacking, entertaining football which would please the fans. He was also a man of immense personal dignity. His genius in 13 years as manager revived Celtic, bringing them success which will never be equalled: 10 league titles (nine of them won consecutively), eight Scottish Cups and six League Cups. He led the side to two European Cup finals, winning the competition in 1967. This was his finest season, when his team won every competition they entered. But unlike Matt **Busby**, whose English side won the cup in 1968, Stein oddly did not receive a knighthood.

Scotland manager He left to manage Leeds United in 1978 but was brought back to take charge of the national side. Again his talents were manifest, this time more steadily and less flamboyantly, when he steered his team to qualification for the 1982 World Cup. Tragically and dramatically, he died at the trackside during a crucial match with Scotland on the point of victory.

The Stevenson Family
18th–20th centuries
Engineers

Engineering is a profession traditionally associated with Scots, with no family more prominent in the field than the Stevensons.

Northern Lighthouse Board The family patriarch was Robert Stevenson (1772–1850). He was a small child when his widowed mother married Thomas Smith, an Edinburgh lampmaker and first engineer of the Northern Lighthouse Board, set up to build new lighthouses and make Scottish coastal waters safer for shipping. Robert followed in his stepfather's career, first as his assistant but eventually as his partner and, in 1808, successor as Lighthouse Board engineer. Robert built over 20 lighthouses, the most famous of which was the ingeniously designed lighthouse on the treacherous Bell Rock off the east coast.

Alan, David and Thomas Robert annually toured the lighthouses, often with his family in tow. Three of his sons – Alan (1807–65), David (1815–86) and Thomas (1818–87) – also became engineers, working both in the Northern Lighthouse Board and in their own firm where they diversified into other areas of civil engineering. Alan built to an innovative design a light at Skerryvore in the difficult Atlantic waters off Tiree, and both he and Thomas (the father of Robert Louis **Stevenson**) were lighthouse optics experts. The brothers also designed lighthouses for waters from Newfoundland to Japan.

Further generations David's sons, David Alan and Charles, followed the family tradition, Charles being particularly interested in the use of wireless in coastal communication. Charles' son, D Alan, carried on the lighthouse work in Scotland and in India. Among his projects was the deepening of the Clyde to accommodate the newly built *Queen Mary* after her launch in 1934. D Alan (d. 1971) was the last of his family to enter the profession.

Robert Louis Stevenson
1850–1894
Writer

Disturbing childhood Robert Lewis Balfour Stevenson was born in Edinburgh, the only child of Thomas **Stevenson**, a son of the famous engineering family, and Margaret Balfour, a minister's daughter. As the child of a well-to-do family, the sickly Lewis was under the care of a loving nanny-cum-nurse; unknown to his protective parents, however, this god-fearing Calvinist wreaked havoc with their imaginative son's psyche by telling bed-time tales frightening enough to induce night terrors in her young charge.

Education Lewis' education was constantly interrupted by his ill-health but he went to Edinburgh University in 1867 to study engineering. (It was during his adolescence that he adopted the French spelling of his name, although the pronunciation never altered.) But by 1871 he had persuaded his stern yet endlessly indulgent father that writing was the career he wished to pursue; as a compromise they settled on the law. He qualified as an advocate in 1875 but never practised.

Rebellious adolescence During Stevenson's student days he adopted the pose of a young dandy-about-town, drinking and debauching in Edinburgh's rank and degenerate Old Town before returning to the bourgeois respectability of his family's New Town home in Heriot Row. The separation of rich and poor in Edinburgh which Stevenson explored was a physical manifestation of the duality which many artists, such as James **Hogg**, perceived to lie at the centre of the Scottish psyche, and it was a question which preoccupied him throughout his life. These were also trying times for his parents and especially for his father, with whom he argued vehemently and whom he shocked by loud protestations of his loss of faith. Nevertheless, his parents, everanxious about his health, continued to finance his travelling to take him from the remorselessly raw Edinburgh winters.

1870s: Early writings and marriage
Stevenson already had a book published by the time he was 16: *The Pentland Rising*, his account of the Covenanters, was paid for by his father. By the late 1870s he was starting to make some money from his reviews and essays, and his  travels abroad for his health gave him material enough for two successful books – *An Inland Voyage* and *Travels with a Donkey in the Cevennes*. While he was in France in 1877 he met and fell in love with Fanny Osborne, a married American woman ten years his senior and with two children. She returned to California to be reconciled with her philandering husband, but when Stevenson heard in 1879 that Fanny was now seeking divorce, he hurried to America to marry her himself. Travel by the cheapest means possible on boat and cross-continental train almost killed him, but several months in the California sunshine encouraged a recovery, and in 1880 he and his new bride and family returned to Scotland. The worries of Stevenson's parents over this latest escapade were happily resolved when they and Fanny took instantly to each other. But the Edinburgh cold soon affected his

lungs again, and Stevenson was soon forced to move on with his new family in tow.

Success and fame Almost all of his most famous work dates from after his marriage. By 1882 he had completed *Treasure Island*, originally written to amuse Lloyd, his stepson. The adventure stories *Kidnapped* and *Catriona* followed, and he also published books of verse. The problem of duality and the co-existence of good and evil are present in all of his novels but are brought out most forcefully in *The Strange Case of Dr Jekyll and Mr Hyde*. Stevenson wrote this most famous of all his tales after being wakened by his wife in the middle of a nightmare, for which he rebuked her. He immediately got up and wrote out the story from his dream. Fanny, however, was dissatisfied, feeling that what was a simple tale of horror could be reworked to reveal a fundamental truth of human nature. Stevenson took her at her word and, to her horror, threw the manuscript onto the fire. The book, published in 1886, was the outcome of the second draft. *Treasure Island* had established his reputation, but *Jekyll and Hyde* catapulted him to fame.

Life in the South Seas In 1887 Stevenson's father died. With this last strong link to Scotland broken he took his family and his mother and left Britain for America. The following year the group chartered a boat in San Francisco and sailed to the South Seas, eventually settling on Samoa where Stevenson bought an estate at Vailima. He loved the island and people, and he became an important figure locally. At the time of his death he was dictating to his stepdaughter *Weir of Hermiston*, from which he rose in mid-sentence to prepare mayonnaise for a salad when he was struck down by a cerebral haemorrhage. This unfinished work, whose every word is finely chosen and every sentence summons vivid pictures and strong emotions, shows a consummate storyteller come to the height of his powers. It is Stevenson's masterpiece and the finest work ever produced by a Scottish writer.

Robert Tannahill
1774–1810
Poet and weaver

Apprentice weaver The son of a silk weaver, Robert Tannahill was
born in Paisley on 3 June 1774. At 13 he left school to become
apprentice to his father. He worked in Lochwinnoch before settling in Bolton in Lancashire at the end of 1799, but the death of
his father in 1802 brought him back to Paisley.

Literary success The hand-loom weavers were among the best-off,
most literate and educated artisans of that time, and they were
advocates of wider education. Tannahill himself read avidly and
widely while working at the loom, and in 1805 he was instrumental in setting up the first library for working men in Paisley.
He was also a member of the local **Burns** club, and read out his
own poems and lyrics to the knowledgeable audience he found
there. His songs began to appear in Glasgow periodicals and some
were set to music, gaining instant popularity. They were published
together in book form in 1807.

His work Many of Tannahill's works are not unlike those of
Burns, whom he admired. His subject matter also ranged widely,
from drinking songs and epitaphs to longer, descriptive poems.
However, his Scottish songs were always his most popular. He
once said that the greatest pleasure he derived from his work was
hearing someone working indoors singing one of his songs as he
walked down a street. Tannahill never married, but his love for
Janet Tennant was celebrated in his songs.

Suicide Tannahill's health was never good – he suffered from TB
– and in 1810 he fell into a depression over difficulties in relations
with his publishers over a new edition of his works. In a fit of
despair he drowned himself in a Paisley canal. He had burned his
manuscripts before his suicide, but copies were held by his friends,
and they were later published in new editions.

Thomas Telford
1757–1834
Engineer

Early hardship The foremost engineer of the Industrial Revolution, Thomas Telford was born to a poor family at Westerkirk in Dumfriesshire. His father died soon after he was born, and as a small child Thomas was obliged to herd cattle for local farmers to bring in money.

Climbing the ladder He received a basic education, although his early lack of learning was something he made up for later in life, eventually teaching himself chemistry, drawing and poetry, in all of which he became proficient. He was apprenticed at 15 to a stonemason and later became a journeyman, wandering the country in search of work: he was in Edinburgh helping build the New Town in 1779; in London in 1782; and in Portsmouth in 1784. A powerful Dumfries patron got Telford the surveyorship of public works for Shropshire, the first job in which he came fully to prominence. His professional and personal popularity were such that in 1793 he was appointed in overall charge of the building of the Ellesmere Canal, distinguishing himself especially in his innovative designs for two aqueducts.

Opening up the Highlands In 1803 Telford was back in Scotland as civil engineer for a huge government scheme to bring a new network of communications to the Highlands. He supervised the building of almost 1000 miles of roads where, apart from military roads, only tracks and paths had existed before; he built hundreds of bridges, great and small, replacing often dangerous local ferries; and he improved harbours, including those at Wick, Peterhead and Aberdeen. His most difficult task was building the Caledonian Canal through the Great Glen, where 60 miles of freshwater lochs were to be linked by 20 miles of canal across hilly countryside. The cost was double the original estimate and the canal was not commercially successful. It remained the one disappointment of his career.

Early suspension bridge At the same time Telford was working in England and Europe where his reputation as the foremost civil engineer of his day was secure.

He was nicknamed 'the Colossus of Roads' by the Poet Laureate.

Telford was responsible for many famous structures across Britain, but one of his most famous is the Menai Bridge at Anglesey. He was one of the few British engineers to use the suspension principle, but so nervous was he over the success of his project that he could not sleep in the last weeks before its completion, and friends arriving to congratulate him on the final day when the chains were to be hoisted into place found him kneeling in prayer.

Selfless nature Telford was a very sociable and popular man, full of fun and with a ready anecdote. For 21 years his base in London was the Salopian Coffee House, and his presence and personality ensured that the premises were always packed to capacity. When Telford announced his intention to move to a house he had just bought, the new landlord complained bitterly, 'Why, sir; I have just paid £750 for you!' He was also a man of principle: despite his success, his estate after his death was found to be worth relatively little, as he often took on unpaid work on projects which were in the public, rather than his own, interest.

Charles Tennant
1768–1838
Chemist

First business venture   Charles Tennant was born at Ochiltree where he was educated first at home, then at the local school. He was apprenticed to a weaver at Kilbarchan to learn silk manufacturing and later moved to a bleachfield at Wellmeadow to study textile bleaching. After learning that business he and a partner set up their own bleachfield at Darnley outside Glasgow.

Opportunities of industrialisation   Textiles was one of the key industries whose requirements were the catalyst for many of the advances of the Industrial Revolution. The chemical industry grew quickly by supplying the textile industry with easier-to-use processes and materials, and it was in this that Tennant saw opportunities. The old method of bleaching cloth had involved leaving it exposed to the elements for several days at a time, but by the end of the 18th century this was being replaced by the use of chemicals. In 1798 Tennant patented a new, cheap, liquid bleach. He was called upon to defend it shortly afterwards, when he took a group of Lancashire bleachers to court for their use of a similar solution. He lost the case when the patent was proved bad on the grounds that the bleachers had been using the process for several years, having arrived at it independently. (There were no lasting hard feelings between Tennant and the Lancashire bleachers – they later presented him with a gift of plate for his services to the bleaching industry.)

Big breakthrough   Success came in 1799, when Tennant patented a bleaching powder, probably devised by a partner, Charles **Macintosh**. This solid mixture had the benefit of portability, and could easily supply the burgeoning British textile industry. In 1800 Tennant and his partners moved to St Rollox, opening a new chemical works which became the largest in the world.

Thomas the Rhymer
Lived in the mid–late 13th century
Poet and seer

Thomas the Rhymer, whose name was supposed to be Learmont, was born and lived at Erceldoune (now Earlston) in Berwickshire. Not a lot of details of his life are known, although he was a real person – his name appears on local charters.

Relationship with the fairies He also appears in the eponymous ballad *Thomas the Rhymer*, which **Scott** included in his collection *Minstrelsy of the Scottish Border*. According to this, Thomas saw the Queen of the Fairies as she was out riding in the Eildon Hills one day. He was captivated by her beauty and they became lovers but he had to return with her to her kingdom inside the hills, where he remained for what seemed to him three days but was actually three years. He was allowed to return to earth but was obliged to return at her summons.

Gift of prophesy The queen as a keepsake gave Thomas the gift of prophesy. Among his predictions were the death of **Alexander III**, the disastrous defeat of **James IV**'s army at Flodden, and the succession of **James VI** to the thrones of Scotland and England. All his prophesies on local and national events, and those attributed to him, were collected together and published for the first time in 1603. Belief in them was so enduring that they were even consulted before the Jacobite risings of 1715 and 1745.

Writings Thomas is also believed to have written the romance *Sir Tristrem*, edited by **Scott** and thought by him to be the oldest piece of Scots poetry.

His return Thomas himself was thought to have returned to the Queen of the Fairies after he walked out of his towerhouse one day and was never seen again. According to legend, he will appear again, like James IV, to come to Scotland's aid in the hour of her greatest need.

William Thompson
1824–1907
Physicist

Youthful talent Although he regarded himself as a Scot, William Thompson was actually Irish, born in Belfast. His mother, who died when he was six, was Scottish, and the family moved to Glasgow in 1832 when his father became mathematics professor at the university. Professor Thompson taught his children himself and when William was 10 he entered the university where he first became interested in natural philosophy. At 16 he went to Cambridge, and at the prodigiously young age of 22 he returned to Glasgow to take up the natural philosophy chair.

Advances in physics Thompson was one of the foremost scientists of his generation and extended his versatile talents to both pure and applied science, believing that 'the life and soul of science is its practical application'. He established a commanding reputation as a mathematical physicist and made discoveries in thermodynamics, hydrodynamics and electricity. He devised the absolute (Kelvin) temperature scale; invented the submarine telegraph cable (personally supervising its laying in the Atlantic); improved marine compasses; and invented electrical instruments (his house was the first to be lit by electricity). As well as his theoretical and practical talents, Thompson remained a teacher and entered a very successful business partnership with a local optical instrument maker, manufacturing many of the 56 measuring instruments Thompson had patented by 1900.

Personal life Thompson was created Lord Kelvin in 1892 and held his chair at Glasgow until 1899. He was married twice: to his cousin, who died in 1870, and to the daughter of a Madeira wine merchant. Both marriages were childless but happy. Thompson's health was not good in his final years – he suffered from neuralgia – and he died of shock after his wife had a stroke.

Alexander 'Greek' Thomson
1817–1875
Architect

Family background   Alexander Thomson was born in Balfron.
His father, a bookkeeper, married twice, and Alexander was the
seventeenth of his 24 children. He first worked in a lawyer's office
where some of his drawings were seen by an architect who took
him as apprentice. In 1834 he joined the practice of John Baird,
going into partnership with him and his son in 1837.

Work and style   Thomson spent his adult life in Glasgow, and it
is there that the majority of his distinctive mature work can be
seen. He designed buildings of all types, from churches and ware-
houses to great houses and tenements. His neo-classical style, with
its fine proportions, distinctive compositions and use of ancient
Eastern motifs, earned him the name 'Greek' Thomson. Among
his finest work still standing is the United Presbyterian church in
St Vincent St, Walmer Crescent, Moray Place (where he himself
lived) and Great Western Terrace. His style was highly popular,
and was copied and adapted by many talented followers. The
result has bequeathed to Glasgow Victorian architecture which is
among the finest in the world and a look which gives the city a
sense of dignity and grandeur.

Missed opportunity   Unfortunately, a certain provincial outlook
in the university establishment cost Glasgow the chance to have a
grand Thomson building for the university's move to its new site
at Gilmorehill. As is often the case in Glasgow, native talent was
overlooked – this time in favour of George Gilbert Scott's plans
for a Glaswegian Gothic revival – much to the scorn of Thomson,
who ridiculed the university's decision.

His talent recognised   Unlike **Mackintosh**, Thomson's work was
not so revolutionary as to disconcert and upset his fellows, and his
genius was acknowledged in his own lifetime.

William Wallace
c. 1270–1305
Patriot

Scotland in the 1290s Scotland was occupied by English forces in the late 1290s after King John Balliol's deposition by Edward I who subsequently regarded himself as overlord of Scotland. But divisions among the Scots leaders – notably between the Bruces and Balliols – made resistance difficult. The spread of the Normans throughout Britain after the Conquest had also blurred lines of national allegiance. Against this background, Wallace's life and achievements seem all the more remarkable.

Catalyst and early successes He was born into a family of minor nobility in Elderslie but little is known of his early life. It is not known if the catalyst for his struggle was the murder by English forces of his father and brother or of his wife, Marion Bradfute, but in May 1297 he and his followers attacked and murdered the English sheriff William Hazelrig at Lanark. He then moved north, harrying English government representatives, and joined forces with Sir Andrew Murray who was waging a similar campaign. In September they won a great victory at Stirling Bridge, defeating the English forces under the Earl of Surrey and Hugh Cressingham, the detested head of the English administration. Such was the Scots' hatred of Cressingham that his body was skinned after the battle and strips are divided up as trophies; Wallace had his portion made into a sword-belt.

Guardian of the country This was his finest moment, and he became Guardian of Scotland in the name of John Balliol. He invaded northern England and recaptured Berwick, his success drawing many to the Scottish cause. But the nobles remained ambivalent – they did not want to follow a man of a lower social standing, and the Bruces were reluctant to fight for Balliol.

Obscurity and betrayal In 1298 Edward came north. He met and defeated Wallace at Falkirk, where the English longbow won the day. Wallace resigned his guardianship and travelled to France in 1299 to try to gain the support of the pope and the French king. The Scots' resistance collapsed quickly, and when Wallace returned in 1303 he was able to wage only a minor guerrilla campaign. With a price on his head, he was betrayed in 1305 by one of his own followers outside Glasgow and handed over to be sent to London for trial.

Trial and execution Wallace was accused of treason, a charge he refuted on the grounds that he had never acknowledged Edward as king and was his enemy, not a rebel. But the trial was a formality, and on 23 August he was dragged in chains through the streets to Smithfield where before a baying crowd he was hanged, cut down before he was dead, disembowelled and quartered; his limbs were sent as a warning to Newcastle, Berwick, Stirling and Perth.

His patriotism Wallace was recognised as a patriotic hero in his own lifetime, and his reputation was enhanced by the 15th-century poem *The Wallace*. He blazed a trail later followed most notably by **Robert** Bruce. He is one of the few to emerge from Scotland's War of Independence with uncompromised honesty and selfless motive, and he stands as Scotland's greatest patriot.

Robert Watson-Watt
1892–1973
Pioneer of radar

Education   Robert Alexander Watson Watt (his name was not hyphenated until later in life) was born in Brechin, the son of a carpenter and a descendant of James **Watt**, pioneer of the steam engine. He was educated at University College, Dundee, and after graduating he worked as a researcher in the Natural Philosophy Department there.

Work in meteorology   In the wake of developments in aviation and the outbreak of the First World War, a way was needed to warn pilots of fragile early planes of approaching thunderstorms, and in 1915 Watson-Watt moved to the meteorology section of the Royal Aircraft Factory at Farnborough to undertake research into radio location of storms. By 1918, storms several hundred miles away could be located accurately. The work interested him, and was not dissimilar to his later work in radio detection and ranging (radar). As a result of his war success, he was moved into radio-location research work, becoming superintendent of the National Physical Laboratory's new radio department by 1933 with responsibility for developing a radar tracking system.

Development of radar   The idea of radar was not new – it had been mooted in a science-fiction novel earlier in the century, and others were also working on its development. However, Watson-Watt's achievement would be in ingeniously devising a system which could operate simply and efficiently in wartime. He worked at secret bases with a dedicated team, and by 1935 he was able to give recommendations for the development of a radar tracking system. The Government was sufficiently convinced to plan a national network of stations to protect the British coast from enemy aircraft. By the end of 1938, a secret system was in place covering the North Sea approaches; it was extended to the whole country by the time war broke out in 1939. The Germans were also known to have made little progress in the field; they had been secretly assessed personally by Watson-Watt and his wife (who became director of the WAAF from 1939 to 1943) who travelled undercover as tourists to Germany in 1937.

Radar's importance for Britain's survival

Radar was the weapon in the critical Battle of Britain in 1940 which allowed the RAF to intercept and shoot down many German aircraft even before they reached British shores. Watson-Watt later ranked the reasons for success as the pilots, the planes, and then radar. His system was essential to Britain's gaining and maintaining mastery of the skies throughout the war and was arguably the single biggest technological factor in the Allied victory.

Later career
Watson-Watt was adviser on telecommunications at the Ministry of Aircraft Production in 1940, and stayed on as a government adviser until 1949. By then his system had been extended to peacetime purposes such as civil air and maritime navigation. He received honours from around the world, including a knighthood in 1942 and, almost uniquely, in recognition of the importance of his pioneering work he was awarded £52,000 by the Government.

James Watt
1736–1819
Pioneer of the steam engine

Childhood talents James Watt was born on 19 January 1736 in Greenock, the fourth of five children. As a child he suffered from poor health and did not attend school regularly. Despite this, he displayed a talent for engineering at an early age, and spent much of his time in his father's workshop, where he made models of pulleys, cranes and even little barrel organs.

Advances in steam engines At the age of 19 he left for London to work without pay and in conditions of poverty as an apprentice instrument-maker. Ill-health forced his return to Glasgow in 1757 where he secured the post of mathematical instrument-maker and repairer at the university. In 1764 Watt was asked to repair the university's Newcomen steam engine. This engine was the best of its type, but was essentially a pump and, without potential for other application, was limited in its use. It was also inefficient in its use of steam. Watt cracked the problem of how to modify the engine as he was taking a Sunday afternoon stroll but, because of the strict Sabbatarianism then in vogue, he waited until Monday to write out his ideas. The answer was to separate the condenser for the used steam (which needed a low temperature to re-convert it into water) from the cylinder (requiring a high temperature to maintain the steam) and enclose the cylinder in a steam jacket.

Production difficulties His colleague, Joseph **Black**, lent him money to patent his separate condenser, and in 1765 he introduced Watt to John Roebuck, an entrepreneur with chemical and iron works. The pair subsequently went into partnership. They experienced production problems, however, and Watt's invention was still to be exploited when Roebuck went bankrupt in 1773.

Commercial success The patent for the engine was bought by a Birmingham entrepreneur, Matthew Boulton, in 1774. Although

Watt's first wife, Margaret, had died in 1773, he took his young family south in 1774 to enter into partnership with Boulton. Their association was a successful one, with Boulton's pragmatic and level-headed approach complementing Watt's highly strung nature and tendency to panic over setbacks. The firm became financially successful in the 1780s, and Watt was able to retire a wealthy man in 1800, by when his and Boulton's sons were running the business.

Interests and achievements Watt continued inventing until his death, devising, among other things, a steam locomotive (which he did not develop), pipe organs, which he played to entertain his friends, and sculpturing machines, a final obsession although not one which outlasted him. Other innovations are also attributed to him: he invented a chemical document copier; he was first to use the term 'horsepower'; he discovered the composition of water; and he continued to develop and improve on his steam engine. During his time as Glasgow University's instrument-maker he had also worked as a surveyor to boost his income, and successfully surveyed many of Scotland's canals. The unit of power, the 'watt', is named after him.

Importance The place of Watt's steam engine in the Industrial Revolution was central: it proved to be the springboard for the modern world, powering the new cotton mills and manufactories, and it allowed Britain to achieve the pre-eminence which it maintained throughout the following century and beyond.

Nora Wattie
1899–1994
Pioneer in social medicine

Nora Wattie is a heroine of the type whose lives have a profound effect on those they touch but who go unrecorded in history. She was a native of the north-east where her mother founded the first nursery school in Aberdeen. She graduated in medicine from Aberdeen in 1921, working in Cambridge and Edinburgh before joining Glasgow's health and welfare department in 1924.

Neonatal care   Her first interest was in ante-natal and neonatal health. She worked tirelessly with pregnant women who had been infected with sexually transmitted diseases by their husbands returning from the war. Consequences for their babies could be tragic, as congenital syphilis caused blindness. In the days before penicillin, the newborns' eyes had to be washed out every hour; the babies could not sleep, and work in the ward was harrowing. Nevertheless, the sight of many babies was saved.

Mother and child health   Dr Wattie became Glasgow's head of maternity and child welfare. The practical measures she took to improve the health of mothers and their families ranged from setting up proper ante-natal clinics and a team of health visitors as a means of reducing infant mortality, to distributing milk and cod-liver oil (bought out of the city's rates in pre-NHS days) to eliminate rickets in poor children. The successful service she built from the 1930s until her retirement in 1964 owed immensely to her talent and enthusiasm, and gained national and international recognition. In addition to working by day, Dr Wattie advised women's guild groups and others on health in the evenings. She continued her advisory work after retirement.

It is difficult today for a professional woman to perform her job and look after her family; earlier this century it was impossible, and Dr Wattie never married.

John Wheatley
1869–1930
Politician

Childhood poverty John Wheatley, born in Co. Waterford, was
not a Scot, but had a huge influence on the Scottish political
scene. As with so many others, his family left Ireland to enable his
father to find work in the Lanarkshire coal mines. John himself
had to leave school at 11 to work in the pits, but kept up his education
through nightclasses. The desperate conditions in which
his family lived, with his parents and 10 sisters and brothers in
one room without water or sanitation, marked him and his politics
throughout his life – as a cabinet minister, he later tried to
ensure that no-one would have to endure what he did.

Business success Wheatley left the pits at 24 and took on a succession
of jobs. He married a publisher's daughter in 1896, and
his father-in-law may have advised him in the printing and publishing
business he began in 1912. It was a success, giving him and
his family financial security and allowing him later to move into
newspaper publishing.

Irish Catholic influence Wheatley was always interested in politics,
and as an Irish Catholic his first allegiance was to the United
Irish League. But in 1910 he joined the ILP, quickly becoming a
force in the party. He founded and led the Catholic Socialist
Society which was influential in leading the Irish Catholic vote in
Scotland away from concern solely with Irish affairs to support for
the Labour Party, a legacy which remains largely intact today. His
achievements were not made without battles with the Church
hierarchy, however, who were deeply suspicious of socialism.

Political success Wheatley became a local councillor in 1909, and
in 1922 he won the Shettleston parliamentary seat for Labour. He
was one of the influential left-wing group known as the Red
Clydesiders who included such figures as James **Maxton**.

Throughout his political life Wheatley was deeply concerned with the twin issues of housing and health, and when he became Minister of Health in the 1924 Labour administration he set about putting into law his ideas for municipal housing. In the Housing Act, also called the Wheatley Act, he gave the Labour Government of 1924 one of its single most effective pieces of administration. The Act gave subsidies to county councils and corporations for house-building; these houses were then rented out at rates affordable to working-class people. It was envisaged that two and a half million homes would be built, and it allowed the building of 75,000 houses in Scotland alone. But Wheatley became disenchanted with parliamentary politics and the **MacDonald** administration, and moved to the backbenches, moving farther leftward politically as time went on. His health was not good, and he died suddenly at the relatively early age of 61.

Conviction socialism Although he was reasonably wealthy at the time of his death (his children, one of whom went on to become a judge, were privately educated, and his family lived comfortably), his financial security never eroded his socialist ideals which came, he said, 'from that spirit of brotherhood which is ever present in the hearts of men but which is often suppressed by the struggle for existence.'

David Wilkie
1785–1841
Artist

Precocious talent David Wilkie was the son of a minister and was born at Cults in Fife. Even as a toddler he had shown a talent for drawing, and his family financed his training at the Trustees' Academy in Edinburgh, the foremost Scottish art school of its day. On his return home in 1804 Wilkie began work almost immediately on what became *Pitlessie Fair*. He used the faces of many of his father's congregation in the work as well as members of his family – although his father was aghast at being depicted chatting with the local publican. He sold the painting and set off for London on the proceeds, to finish his training. The first painting of his London career, *The Village Politicians*, was exhibited at the Royal Academy exhibition of 1806 and caused a sensation, making Wilkie famous overnight.

A bad year Wilkie earned a good living in London as a genre painter of domestic scenes. His health was always fragile, however; he fell ill through overwork in 1811, and he suffered a complete breakdown in 1825 after a series of tragedies which saw the deaths within months of his mother, two brothers and the fiancé of his favourite sister on the eve of her wedding.

Change in style The years Wilkie spent abroad recuperating in Italy and Spain had a great influence on his painting, which on his return in 1828 was modelled on the style of the great masters such as Velasquez. But the change was not popular with his public, and despite royal patronage he never again reached the heights of popularity he had enjoyed in his early career. Ill health forced him abroad once more in 1840, this time to the Holy Land, where he completed a set of what are arguably his best sketches. He died on the voyage home and was buried at sea near Malta in a scene depicted by his friend J. M. W. Turner, in *Peace: Burial at Sea*.

Peter Williamson
1730–1799
Adventurer

Kidnapped The title of 'adventurer' is scarcely adequate for someone who packed so many experiences into his life as Peter Williamson. Born the son of a crofter at Aboyne, he was kidnapped from the Aberdeen quayside when he was 10, shipped across the sea and sold for £16 into slavery in America.

Mixed fortunes He gained his freedom when he was 17 and later married the daughter of a local landowner. His luck did not last, however; his home was burnt down in a night-time raid by Indians and he was held prisoner by them for months. When he escaped he thought his new-found knowledge of the Indians could be put to best use in the army, but he was soon captured by the French who held him as a prisoner of war in Quebec. He was finally discharged from the army in 1757 at Plymouth on account of a hand wound, with six shillings in his pocket.

Aberdonian displeasure Williamson wrote an account of all his adventures which proved popular everywhere except Aberdeen; the city was then notorious because of official connivance in the kidnapping trade, and local merchants were furious at being accused. On his return home in 1758 he was sued for libel, banished from the city and had his book burned. (He had the last laugh when he won £100 in a counter-suit four years later; he also successfully sued those involved in the kidnapping trade.)

Success Williamson settled in Edinburgh where he became a local character, opening a popular tavern called 'Indian Peter's Coffee Room' in Parliament House. He started a penny post which was taken over by the GPO in 1791, earning him a £25 annual pension; he published the city's first street directory; and dreamed up diverse inventions, from a labour-saving harvesting device to a pack of cards which divined a person's thoughts.

James Young
1811–1883
Discoverer of paraffin

Academic success James Young was born in Glasgow. The son of a joiner, he worked with his father by day and studied chemistry at night in Anderson's College, alongside David **Livingstone** and the scientist Lyon Playfair, both of whom became lifelong friends. Young was a successful student, and in the 1831–32 term he was appointed assistant to his professor, Thomas Graham. He left Glasgow with him when Graham went to University College, London, in 1837.

Paraffin manufacture In 1839, through Graham's influence, Young became chemist at an alkali works in Manchester. But in 1847 he received a letter from his old friend Playfair telling him of a petroleum spring which belonged to his brother-in-law in Derbyshire, and suggesting that Young might be able to use it. He and a partner bought the rights to the spring, from which they manufactured illuminating and lubricating oils. The spring dried up in 1851, but by then Young had devised and patented a process of manufacturing paraffin from coal. He entered into partnership with a Glasgow businessman to extract oils from coal at Bathgate, first producing naphtha and lubricating oils, then paraffin when demand grew sufficiently from 1856. Young successfully defended his patent in court several times. He bought out his partners in 1865, opened a second works at Addiewell, and sold the lot the following year for £400,000.

Personal wealth Young made other discoveries in the field of industrial chemistry, all of which left him a wealthy man with more than enough for himself and his family of seven children. However, he was not selfish with his money: he honoured all of Livingstone's debts on his African trips, and in 1870 he endowed the Young Chair at Anderson's College for £10,500.

Index of personalities by profession

COLLINS GEM

Bestselling Collins Gem titles include:

Gem English Dictionary (£3.50)

Gem Calorie Counter (£2.99)

Gem Thesaurus (£2.99)

Gem French Dictionary (£3.50)

Gem German Dictionary (£3.50)

Gem Basic Facts Mathematics (£3.50)

Gem Birds Photoguide (£3.99)

Gem Babies' Names (£2.99)

Gem Card Games (£3.50)

Gem World Atlas (£3.50)

COLLINS